The Journey Of An Overcomer

Memoirs from The Heart Of A Little Girl

Copyright © 2025 Edna Ercille Sanders

Living Water Book Publishing Co, LLC
Little Rock, Arkansas
Livingwaterbooks.org

The Library of Congress has cataloged the previous editions as follows: Edna Sanders. The Journey Of An Overcomer - New Paperback Print Book Edition 2025

ISBN 979-8-9987543-0-2

All rights reserved. This book is protected by the copyright laws of the United States of America. This book may not be copied or reprinted for commercial gain or profit. Any portion thereof may not be reproduced or used in any manner whatsoever without the express written permission of Edna Ercille Sanders except for the use of brief quotations in a book review or occasional page copying for personal or group study is also allowed and encouraged.

The information contained in this book is intended for information purposes only and should not be construed as legal advice on any subject matter. You should not act or refrain from acting based on any content included in this book without seeking legal or other professional advice. To the best of my ability, I have shared events, locales, people, and organizations from my memories of them. In order to maintain the anonymity of others, in some instances, I have changed the names of individuals and places, and the details of events. I have also changed some identifying characteristics, such as physical descriptions, occupations, and places of residence. Most names and identifying details have been changed to protect individuals' privacy.

Unless otherwise indicated, Scripture quotations are from the Holy Bible New King James Version NKJV copyright 1973, 1978, 1984. Used by permission of Zondervan. All Rights Reserved

The Journey
Of An Overcomer

Memoirs from The Heart Of A Little Girl

Edna Ercille Sanders

Dedication

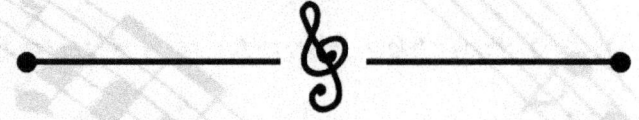

A special dedication to my children, Braisly, Kinslee, Charity, Trinity, Daniel III, and Patrick Reid. Whenever you read this book, I pray that you find the strength to overcome any obstacle. Let my story be a guide for you!

A special dedication to my readers, I pray that you find the help that you need through these pages, the peace of God through my words, I pray that you find yourself through the truth revealed from God's heart.

YOU'RE FINALLY SINGING

Author Edna Sanders

Table of Contents

Dedication 4

Introduction
Your Story Heals 9

Chapter One
Overcome By Your Testimony 19

Chapter Two
Overcoming The Elephant In The Room 23

Chapter Three
The Awakening Of My Calling 41

My Letter To My Dad 52

Chapter Four
Masquerading behind a Toxic Love and an Unhealed Life ... 57

My Letter to My Ex-Husband 75

Chapter Five
Self-Discovery Through My Parenting Style 77

My Letter To My Mom 85

Chapter Six

Changing My Mindset 90

Chapter Seven

Changing My Actions 97

My Letter to Myself 101

Tributes 105

BONUS CONTENT: HEALING JOURNEY

Healing Journey
....108

Poisonous Love Poem
....116

Professional Acknowledgments……………...………………….…..119

Author Biography
…………………………………………………...120

Introduction

Your Story Heals

My mother said, "Edna, I want you to take five giant kangaroo hops." I asked, "Mother, may I?"

Mother said, "Yes, you may." With so much confidence and the biggest smile on my face, I counted loudly every hop of the way. I hopped with all my 4-year-old might. I... 2.. 3…4…. I did it! I was so proud of myself. I can recall many memories of youthful, innocent fun and excitement. I was always so competitive, silly, playful, chatty, carefree, and innocent. As a child, I genuinely enjoyed my outside time, I really enjoyed it because I had a squad to play with all the time! In our free time, my siblings and I would play many childhood games such as: freeze tag, four square, kickball-baseball, hide and seek, dodgeball, wrestling, pile-on… You name it, and oh, my goodness, we did it! We would even make up games or compete to see who could do a chore the fastest. We had so much fun together. These were enjoyable moments we'd share as a family. Occasionally, our parents would join in these games with us. but for the most part, it was just us siblings, cousins, and friends. Although we'd have fun times together, those days seemed to be a mask to cover the secret life that no little girl or any person would ever want to think of. This secret seemed to be the seed that birthed so many dirty-handed lingering thoughts. I cannot recall when my thoughts transitioned or my emotions changed from innocent, excited, fun-focused, and carefree.... But it did. All I know is that I was playing in my room, having fun with my baby dolls and stuffed animals, trying to make them kiss. This was normal for any little girl, right? This was totally innocent until a memory from my head became an idea, and I thought, why not have my dolls pressing each other's private parts?

I shouldn't know this at such a young age, right?

Did she watch it on television?

That has to be the question you must be asking yourself, right?

The truth is, there are many memories lodged into my brain and buried in my soul that I didn't place there. One day, those noticeably confident giant kangaroo hops turned into fearful flops, cowardly crawls, shameful steps, multiple sways of low self-esteem, depression, anger, and anxiety. Yes, there have been numerous times in my life when I've carried these emotions and many more. This book is a testimony of it all and how I became an overcomer. My desire for this book is to help anyone who may be currently feeling overwhelmed with emotions, due to all of life's unique situations. Let my transparency help you to be free!

Disclaimer: Laughter has helped me overcome many situations in my life. So, within the pages of my book, I will use some comical (possibly even some sarcastic remarks. There will be many laugh-out loud (lol) moments, but some very upsetting truths because many issues I mention in the pages are not comical situations.

So let's continue.... I attended a Head Start program in Malvern, Arkansas, and I enjoyed the teachers so much that many of my reasons for wanting to be a teacher stemmed from the teachers in my life. These teachers were Mrs. Womack, Mrs. Vicky, Mrs. Ruby, and most definitely my grandmother, Ercille Devine (I'll talk about her later!) These ladies were cornerstones for me. I needed a place to be safe and free, and they allowed me that space.

As a child, I was abused physically, sexually, mentally, and emotionally. I admit I wasn't the nicest child.... Some of those same teachers may agree that I had some disobedient moments, but I was only a 4-year-old child. The little girl on the cover of this book was (is) me while attending pre-school (in the Head-Start program). Yes, that was me, Edna, so wild, so free, testing limits and disturbing the peace, (lol)! I was content in this 4-year-old world of mine, just being me!

- Was my behavior a result of a child's re-enactment of traumatic events?
- Did I have a bold strength that was just misdirected?
- Or was I really just a bad child?

I can recall one memory of little Edna in her oh so sassy, Head Start years. On this particular day, I decided to tell my teacher to shut up. OMG! (hand on forehead emoji) What was I thinking? Well, I got beat! My daddy tore my butt up…. Yeah, as a mom now, I can see myself handing out a good old-fashioned hand-to-bottom spanking to my 6-year-old son, reminding him to watch his little mouth. I can see myself definitely taking away his screen time and possibly saying, something like "no sweets for you today, little buddy"….

Yeah, well, that's not what happened in my case….

Oh no, daddy, said (niggah-nawl! Lol). He decided to go with an extension cord for his weapon of choice, and well, let's just say I wasn't too quick to say shut up to an adult…. (although, I eventually said worse). The next day at school, that same head start center eventually had to call the Department of Children and Family Services to come see about this little sassy mouth, Edna, who refused to sit down.

No, she wasn't sassy; she was in pain as she yelled out no… my butt hurts! When they finally escorted her to the restroom she noticed the gasps in their voices, the tears in their eyes, and the change of the tones in their voices as they watched her raise her dress to show them why her butt hurt. Little Edna's 4-year-old backside was filled with welts and bruises that were still bleeding from the lashes of the extension cord whipping from her daddy.

My point now is this: Did I deserve it, or was there more misplaced anger taken out on me? I believe this was one of many seeds planted, intended to provoke respect and fear for adults, so I'd remain quiet when the unthinkable occurred. One unthinkable thing that holds so much shame, in my 4-year-old brain…is remembering how a sheet/blanket/robe/gown (a covering of some sort) was thrown over my head; being told to open my mouth…… and I better not bite.

What happened to the little girl within me?

So many memories lodged into my mind… How did I make it out to stand here today to share my story? With tears in my eyes, I survived.

I hope to help that person who (for too many reasons to mention) can't seem to get out of the funk of past and present hurt. This is for anyone needing to come face-to-face with traumatic situations. While reading, I want you to reflect on your past, examine your present, and prepare for your future. Yes, you've had many trials (I want to hear about them). You will have more, but don't fret! My brother, my sister, my friend…. I want you to take one giant step of forgiveness, one giant step of trusting God within you, and one giant step towards overcoming. No need to ask, "Father or Mother, may I?"

It's already in you, (but, if you need to hear it) Yes, you may. Let's overcome together!

Take one giant step of forgiveness,

one giant step of trusting God within you

, and one giant step of overcoming…

Your Story heals...

My conversations with God are a little different than what I hear from most. I think God deals with everyone in God's own way, according to the person. Now listen, I'm ecstatic that God knows me like he does! I'm so grateful that the method of conversation we have together works for who? Me! See y'all don't understand, I am a scaredy cat when it comes to: ghost, sprits, creators of the unknown etc. not just that, I'm not even a fan of surprises and being caught off guard… yeah, I would not respond well to a big giant voice calling my name saying **Edna, This is God… do this and do that!** Yeah, no I would probably have a massive heart attack somewhere from fear or something. I've realized that I'm not as trusting as I probably should be, so unfortunately, experience has been the leading teacher for me..(hand on head emoji, again!) Thankfully, in God's (IEP-method) of teaching Edna, which transfers in my thoughts as an (Individualized Edna Plan) …(look, we all learn differently), God spoke to me so simply as I was typing out my thoughts….

By simply saying, **God speaks to me**

Edna, my daughter, made in my image, how unique you are! (He likes to butter me up.) LOL. God knows how to talk to me. (LOL) Apparently, I love words of affirmation, and God knows it.

You are great, and yes, it is true, you have been hurt. But listen; you did not go through just for the sake of going through. You went through to help someone else. You went through, and now I need you to share your story with someone else who is quiet and holding their stories in. Be a guide, be a teacher, be ready to listen, be ready to: cry, laugh, and help. You will show others there's a way to forgive and heal after abuse......There's purpose behind this!

So, I am sharing with you, it's not about me and it's not about you! It's about the purpose. Healing is the purpose. When God told me that I didn't go through it just for the sake of going through it, that it was bigger than me, I said to myself, "Edna, you must heal. You must overcome this stepping stone to help the next generation and eventually lead others across. Look, I have to overcome. I must heal. I must help someone else! I must walk into my future without being fearful of my past and present hurtful situations. Today I know that I am an overcomer of rape, sexual assault, self-hate, divorce, and abuse of all sorts. I am being totally healed and delivered as I write to you.

Part One

Overcoming The Past

Reflecting and acknowledging my past and present hurt

Journey of An Overcomer

Listen to "Overcome" by the Clark Sisters

    Instructions:

Get your phone out, open your camera app, and point your camera toward my QR code below. Once the link comes up on your screen, just click it and go directly to the YouTube channel to hear this song. I want you to play this song while you read the section.

THEY WERE OVERCOME BY THE WORD OF THEIR TESTIMONY!

Author Edna Sanders

Journey of An Overcomer

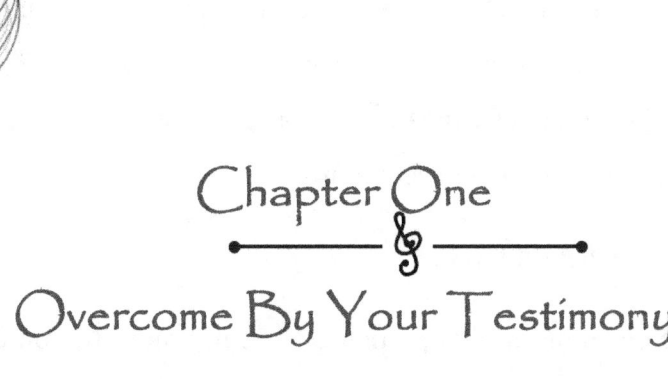

Chapter One
Overcome By Your Testimony

The smell of 409, pine sol, and bleach lingered in the air as I stood in our living room, just doing our regular Saturday morning chores that Momma told us to do. My siblings and I would always sing or play gospel music while doing chores. We grew up in the church, around the church, and through the church, so we sang gospel music all the time. On top of that, my daddy was a pastor, his daddy was a pastor, and so was my mother's daddy.

My siblings and I would make songs up or sing a familiar song just from hearing one word. For example, if someone were to say What's the time? Trust me one of us would sing something like: ***"It's time to make a change, we are the people who can do it"*** *(It's time, by The Winans)* or ***"Time, Time, Time won't be long……."*** *(Unknown artist – sung in old school black gospel churches.)* We just loved to sing, and we loved music.

My mom and dad's sides of the family are both musically inclined. Growing up with a firm Christian believing family, listening to anything that was not Christian or gospel was a no-go. Even some of the church songs we would listen to "**bet-not**" have had a non-gospel sound to them! Shoot, we would sneak just to listen to: "**Do You Want a Revolution**" and "**Stomp**" - by **Kirk Franklin**. So, you know, we shouldn't have even known anything about other secular artists.

But let me get back on topic.

While cleaning up this particular day, my mom put on one of her favorite records. I didn't know then that I would grow to love this song just as much as her, but it stuck with me. She put on this old-school Clark Sisters record. (*Thanks, Mom, for bumping that good Gospel music*) Honestly, I was probably annoyed; annoyed with having to wake up every Saturday morning and deep clean the house. God forbid if it were spring break; (not) a weeklong spring-cleaning session! God-Have-Mercy! Momma! So…. I could care less what they were saying on the music box then. I liked music, and those ladies sounded pretty good, so I just listened and cleaned. However, it was this one song that came on that kind of struck an interest.

(Now listen! I'm not going to lie and act like I remember the exact date, time,) All I know is that, at that time, I do recall stopping to listen to the actual words of the song.

I recall the words because the preachers back then ….. would tell all of the new converts:

Journey of An Overcomer

> *"Tell what happened to you on the altar!*
> *They were overcome by the words of their testimony!*
> *Tell about what God done for you tonight"!*

-A.W. Devine (recalling a quote from my grandpa)

I liked the song, yes, because of the music and the beats. I also liked the fact that it made me think. No, I didn't start living differently right after that……. All I know is that it stopped me in my tracks for a moment and made me think. The song I heard that day was "They Were Overcome" (by The Word) from The Clark Sisters.

In the Bible, Revelation 12:6 states,

> *"And they overcame him by the blood of the lamb*
> *and by the words of their testimony."*

I remember this scripture being preached around me. As I matured and experienced life, this scripture and that song resonated in my soul. The more I thought, oh no, I can't tell this, they don't want to hear that, no one would believe this, don't testify about that, … the more I limited God in my life! I spent time wondering what my testimony should sound like and what an overcomer looks like. Merriam-webster defines overcomer as

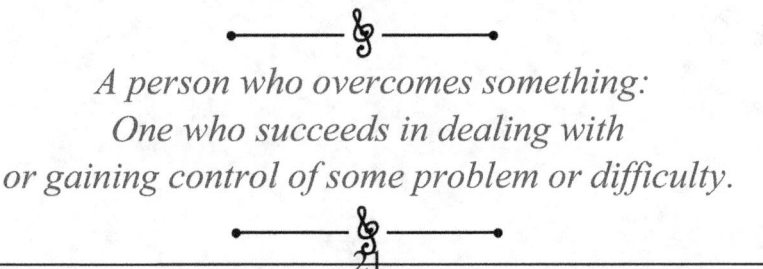

A person who overcomes something:
One who succeeds in dealing with
or gaining control of some problem or difficulty.

We all face some problems or difficulties in our lives. It is inevitable! Inevitable is defined as being incapable of being avoided or evaded. It is inevitable to go through this life without facing some kind of obstacle, problem, or conflict. Job 14:1 states, "Man, that is born of a woman, is of few days and full of trouble." However, in the same book and prior chapter, Job 13:15, says "Though he slay me, yet will I trust in him." I see it this way: that even though I am born into trouble, I will still trust God! Overcomers will have some kind of hurt or heartbreak in this life. It will happen; it is inevitable! Yet even though it is going to happen, I still trust God.

Overcomers trust God to help them through any and every situation. Not only will God help me, but God will help me to be a guiding light to help others. However, I can only do it if I trust God and his process. The song kept playing over and over in my head that day. You may continue to listen to the song as you read my book so that you can relate to being an overcomer!

Chapter Two

Overcoming The Elephant In The Room

    I don't know if you remember, but some years back, there was a broadcast of a local pastor here in Arkansas getting ready for a trial due to the sexual misconduct of a minor who was a member of his church. The reporter went on to mention that one of his daughters (yours truly) turned him in and admitted that she had lived through the same stuff growing up in the home with her biological father. (Yes, I did!) So yes, I am tackling this demon, stronghold, generational curse, or whatever you would like to call it…. because I have been walking around long enough like it's got me ducking my tail between my legs as though I'm ashamed. Nope, not today! (As you see, my whole tone changed)

As an ol' church mother who was so dear to my heart (may she rest in peace) would say) "Ain't no pussy-foot'in around with satan." Listen, this is a book about overcoming. This may hurt or shame some family, or church family, but it's my story., I'm going to tell my story with no apologies for the truth I lived in. If it hurts you too much to read it, imagine actually living it. I am not here to down my dad or my family. I am only here to explain what happened in my past. These things have helped shape my present (good or bad), which is helping me to grow and have a wonderful and victorious future. So, as I was saying, the things I turned him in for are the things I endured as a child. So as a child, I craved my daddy's positive attention. I wanted to be his princess, and I loved it when he would call me his pretty girl, or when he would want a hug. I just loved it whenever he was in a good mood!

Disclaimer: *This section is a bit graphic, read at your own risk*

I loved my daddy and still do, but as a young child, this same daddy turned out to have a different side. One moment, I would be his pretty little girl, and the next hour, I would be his stupid child. It seemed that I was always messing up something. I was trying to be perfect, but I couldn't seem to get it together; I guess in the moments when I was a bad kid to him, he needed to teach me a lesson. During moments like this, Daddy decided to override self-control or self-discipline (whatever you would call it) and prep his children, his daughters, for his own sexual desires.

Whew (deep sigh), okay, let me get myself together emotionally.

He initially started prepping us; and by prepping, I mean that he made me get totally undressed to beat my butt when I got in trouble at school or something. This sounds normal, right? Who remembers the old sayings (I ain't gonna tear up the clothes I bought, etc)? This was his excuse for undressing me and whipping me.

The 2nd way of prepping me is that he began lying on top of me, asking me if he was too heavy. I recall being as young as a child in 3rd and 4th grade. I recall this time so vividly because I was at Fields Elementary. My teachers were unique. I was in Mrs. Coston's (3rd grade), Mrs. Franks and Morris's 4th grade classes. I often got in trouble and had to write sentences because of my behavior. My dad would often pull me into his room to whoop me, but it was a distraction to my mom and the rest of my siblings. While we were in the room, he would tell me to take off all of my clothes. Yes, the whooping's still happened eventually. If not, that would have messed up the charade, right? This went right along with his prepping shenanigans. I would start undressing quickly, but he'd tell me to do it slowly... confused and scared at the same time, I did exactly what he said.

Jesus help me!

My daddy would tell me to show him my breast, then he would lie on top of me. He'd then ask me crazy questions such as:

Am I heavy?

Am I hurting you?

Do you feel that? (stuff like that) (weird right!) Yeah, I know!

He'd whoop my butt for cutting up in school, signing my d-hall slips, cussing out teachers, lying, fighting, etc. and I couldn't explain to any of the teachers that I was doing this to get your attention. Something is happening to me at home, and I need someone to believe me. I was just getting in trouble at school, then I'd get in trouble with him. I was bad, but I had no other way to release the pain.

The 3rd stage of prepping was making my mom go on long errands and/or have her go pick up members for church. He needed enough time to discipline me, but really it was to abuse me sexually. He would tell me to check to see if Momma was gone, and I'd procrastinate as long as I could on returning. Many times, my mom would even be sick at home, suffering from a major illness she was trying to recover from. Yet, he'd have us (my sister and I) doing this same charade (that quickly escalated into full penetration) in his church office where he pastored in England, Ar.

The little girl in me cried every time my mom had to leave

Momma,

    Mommy,

        Mom.......

I'd be crying out, take me with you! I'm crying for you because I feel safe with you! Momma, do you hear my silent cry? Do you know what he's doing to me? Do you care? Did you tell him to do this to me? Would you have protected me if you had known sooner?

I'd go back into my mind over and over because I could see the blue Buick pulling out of the driveway. All along, I wished I were in the car with my mom and my siblings who were with her. On other occasions, it would be the tannish pinkish Cadillac or the navy blue-white Cadillac, then, in my older age, it was the big church vans. There was always a different vehicle for my mom to drive, but the same emotion of my mom leaving me in the hands of a monster. I just wanted to go with her. I needed to be with my mom.

    I recall on multiple occasions, Daddy would send Momma to run numerous errands. She'd be in charge of picking up the church members and taking them home. All six of us children would run to the vehicle to travel with her, but Momma would choose the child or children who could ride with her. The rest of us would either cry or try to find a way to stay as far away from Daddy as possible.

However, that didn't last long. He'd eventually call one of us girls back to his room of choice and have his way. Until the inevitable happened, and on this day, there was nothing I could do to go back to being daddy's little girl.

LET'S TALK ABOUT IT

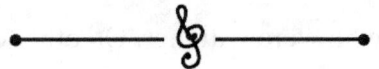

The day the inevitable happened was one afternoon in the Spring, 10-year-old Edna, who was so wild and so free, ran home from the bus stop. I had a fun day at school this day. I recall even seeing a few of my siblings playing outside in the backyard as I ran down Babcock St. I was ready to play with them! Yet, this young Edna had a new obstacle to cross. I was going to have to experience a new pain. On this day, the desire to be daddy's little girl had long gone, and on this day, I never wanted to be his little girl ever again."

As I began playing with my siblings, I heard a yell from my parents' back window. It was my dad, yelling, Edna, come here! I stopped playing, feeling a little worried and thinking what did I do this time? Did one of my teachers call him? His voice sounds so mad. As I hurry and run to him, I recall passing my older sister up as she enters the family bathroom. I see tears in her eyes. My thoughts were confirmed, yeah, I must be getting a whopping, like she just did…As I enter his bedroom, he comes behind me and locks the door. He instantly says, "Why did the school call me today. I was dumb founded because I had actually had a great day. He then says, "No, they didn't call, I just wanted to see if you were going to tell on yourself."

Disclaimer: This is Graphic.
The Inevitable….

Daddy: Lay across the bed

Me: I lay down on my stomach as if I am getting ready for him to whoop my butt.

Daddy: No, turn the other way…

Me: I'm still confused and lost…

Daddy: He then physically turned me on my back and said, "Open your legs."

Me: I put my hands between my legs to cover my privates.

Daddy: Move your hands, I'm your daddy and your mom told me to check you. (He starts asking those same weird questions he'd ask while prepping me. Am I heavy? Has anyone ever touched you like this? He then starts touching me, and of course, I say "No sir." He then says, Close your eyes; tell me if this hurts?

 He inserts a finger, and I yell and start crying. He says, Shut up, do you want me to whoop you? He held a pillow over my face to muffle my screams… Then he inserts his penis, inside of my vagina.

Me: When I could talk, I gasped for air and let out a "Daddy, I'm sorry. Forgive me, Daddy!" He continues to muffle my words and my cries.

While doing this, he'll occasionally take a break to yell out of his window to my siblings, not to don't come into the house, and to start doing various outdoor chores, etc. After one break, he said..

Daddy: Get up, go to the bathroom. I instantly rushed up from his bed and rushed towards his bedroom door to go to our family bathroom. He yells...

Daddy: Where do you think you're going? I didn't tell you to leave! Stupid! I meant my bathroom!

Daddy: Now, bend over the toilet...

Me: Once again, I'm just stiff and scared.... I freeze.

Daddy: He forcibly bends me over the bathroom toilet and tells me over and over don't you ever talk about this... You better not tell anyone; do you want to lose your brothers and sisters? Well, as he proceeds to handle his business, (I guessed mistakenly) he inserts his penis into my butt, but quickly (he must have felt a tad bit of remorse, (definite rolling-eye emoji!!) as I let out the most hideous scream! Sorry, baby, I didn't mean to do that... but then he hits me in the face for screaming.

He then continues with inserting his penis in and out of my 10-year-old vagina..... as he concludes he gives his little spill and say... "Your momma wanted me to check you. (I don't know about you, but I definitely need to go: pray, drink, run, or box, after reliving this)

YOUR MOMMA WANTED ME TO CHECK

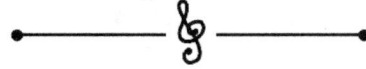

"Hurry up, stop that crying, get dressed, and pull up your clothes! Don't you say anything about this? Your momma wanted me to check to see if you were still a virgin.... I said, "A what? What is that?" He said, "Pull up your clothes and stop crying now."

Slowly walking away and gasping for air…

My thoughts weren't coming to me fast enough. I didn't understand, and the little girl in me thought my momma was in on this, too. I heard him in my head again saying, "Your momma wanted me to check to see if you were still a virgin." That was it for me, in that moment, I just stopped fighting and wishing for Momma to know… It was obvious that she knew and didn't care about me.
I'm finally in the family bathroom alone; I put both of my small hands over my mouth to muffle a screaming cry. That was it…I broke down. He killed me that day. Tears stung my eyes and streamed down my cheeks. Over and over, I kept hearing "Stop crying." his voice rang in my ear as I was shivering, but I couldn't stop crying." My body was numb, and I could barely get undressed. I turned the water on to wash away the stains of his touch. As I attempted to sit in the tub, my privates hit the water. I quickly jumped up and out of the water to grab my towel. Instantly, I fell

to the floor on my knees, holding my privates with the towel, as if in a fetal position.

Why, Daddy, why?
Why did you do this to me? Why?

I was hurting so bad… the pain shattered my soul. I was hurting so bad that my insides stung. I eventually stood up to pee, and that burned like hell.....Then I wiped. I looked again, and my heart dropped because this is when I first noticed blood. I looked to see if it was on the towel, and sure enough, it was bright red like a cherry. I knew a little bit about girls beginning a cycle, but I knew it hadn't started yet. I was only 10 years old. He took my virginity and continued sexually abusing me until I was seventeen years old. He did this as often as he wanted, when he wanted, and anywhere he wanted. Let's name a few places: fishing lake, car, church van, our house, (parents' bedroom, my bedroom, brother's bedroom, hallway floor, living room, bathroom), and the church house.

Did she say that? He did it at church?

Yes, I said it, and yes, he did it! Just keep reading. It had become so regular that regardless of my behavior at home or school, this was done. It was all his choice, and we (my sister and I) never knew when he wanted to do it. During all this time, I would of course put on a smile to make it through the school years. I would laugh, fight, eat, or just sleep my way through the day. I recall one time my mom was leaving, and Daddy called my name.

Dad: Edna, is your momma gone?

Me: sadly, looking out the front window, yes sir…..

Dad: Where are your brothers?

Me: Outside cleaning fish…. Do you want me to go get them?

Dad: No! Lock the doors and come here.

I slowly locked the doors and headed down the hallway of our small 3-bedroom house. Although the house was small, as I walked down the hall, I imagined the hall was as long as the halls in the castle in the Beauty and the Beast movie. There, I imagined that my thoughts would save me… that maybe my imagination would make the hallway longer, the phone would ring, or my brother would pound on the door. As I walked, I thought many thoughts, like. What room today? I hope he doesn't use a pillow because I couldn't breathe the last time. Does he know I have asthma? (tears) Who's gonna save me if I stop breathing?

Well before I knew it, I was standing in front of him.. and he said, "Go in your room, take 'em off, then bend over the bed… He proceeded to insert his thang-thang inside of my vagina and handle his business… I would cry, zone out, and just focus on my breathing so I wouldn't die from my head being pushed into the pillow. I would scream or gasp for air.

One particular day, while he was in mid-stroke (heck, I don't know the proper term) but my mom ran through the house screaming Honey! Honey! Honey! He immediately yanked me up and pushed me in the closet located directly behind him, closed the door, and quickly went to meet her. While inside the closet, I was praying. Lord, please make him stop. I was wondering if maybe this is the chance. Did she see him? Hmmm, well, if she did, maybe we'll all go live with Grandma Devine.

Wishful thinking???

Yeah, let's be real, she'll make me stay with him and accuse me of somehow being at fault. Before I knew it, he was back in the room opening the closet door…. He said, "Get up, lie on your back this time." Yeah, so he continued where he left off. He always had a reason for taking everything from me. He wasn't a man of God, yet he still wanted us to pretend like he was holy and righteous.

ADAPTING THROUGH SERVICES

"Just in case you were wondering how church services would go after, and during all of this? Well, I basically played charades. If you recall, I loved playing games as a child, so I just made my mind pretend while at church. I would build up my childhood thoughts and just trick the little girl inside of me that I'm playing a game of charades. Playing charades to survive church services had become so routine. Eventually, I learned how to attend church and act like nothing ever happened. Isn't that funny?

We're going to church every day where they are teaching us to be so real, while you're teaching me to be so fake… (no, it's actually very sad, and detrimental when raising a generation.)

Once again, I got sidetracked.

The cheerful little girl you met in the introduction started developing into a young lady who just didn't care. As I look back at this moment and relive my emotions, it's hard. It's hard to resurrect old emotions and hidden feelings from a deep, dark grave. Oh, Daddy, I forgive you, and Daddy, I love you, hidden behind fake smiles, forced hugs, and kisses. It was hidden under mounds of let's not make him look bad, and don't even think of messing up the family name, following various religious (man-made) doctrines, and heaps of manipulation, along with brainwashing strategies for many years. I buried the purest form of myself and replaced it with other people's mess.

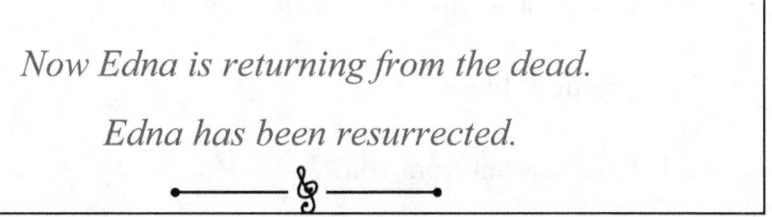

Now Edna is returning from the dead.

Edna has been resurrected.

See, my virginity was snatched from me! He took my virginity, and everyone wanted me just to be quiet and take it. I had my virginity taken before I even started my first cycle! So, if I sound a little angry about that fact, then, oh well! I was a little girl. None of this was my choice. Nobody cared enough to ask me how I was doing, so I became a full-throttle version of "I don't care." I got the I don't care attitude and survived my young life, adolescence, teenage life, and young adulthood on a wing and a prayer. I just did enough to make him happy, but I wanted to do Edna. So I told myself (disclaimer- cover your ears/eyes)

> *If this niggah, gone do what he want to do to me;*
> *then I'm about to do who and what I want to do.*
> *(full inward Edna voice) (As I clap my hands!)*

As I continue, I won't tell you about every encounter with my dad, to spare you and myself, because my stomach is in knots as I write this book. There was a very significant moment that happened that I must share because it is a critical piece. A particular situation occurred where some boys came to our house while Daddy was off preaching somewhere. Yes, that's right, I didn't care, but somehow, Daddy found out about it and, of course, he whipped us when he made it home. A day or so later, he started asking me about the encounter with the boy.

He asked questions like:

What did he want from you?

Did you do what he wanted you to do?

Then he said, "Show me"…. (I'm like, wait-what? You gotta be outta- yo got-damned mind!) Yeah, this man was getting turned on by me telling him what I encountered. He then woke me up later that night and took me behind the house and made me go down on him.

Wait.... I have to pause!

I understand I am writing this book to release the little girl and all the unresolved pain, but as I write this book, I have to relive it. I relive every line, emotion, and memory, so I have to pause, and I pray that you do too! I became more secretive about anything and all things! I was bothered by boys and men who were not my family, and I could not tell Daddy. Do you know what it's like to have a dad you can't run to, but they are teaching me the word of God? Do you see how dysfunctional this is? I could not and would not tell anyone. I assumed that He would make me do it (whatever it was to him) I just assumed that all men were like that, and for the longest, I felt that everyone's dad, uncle, cousin, preacher etc., was hurting someone close to them.

So, guess what happened?

I became promiscuous. I did stuff with whom I wanted, and that's that. I just didn't care anymore. I even experimented with girls, but I realized very quickly that I LOVE MEN! The older saints, and or some family members, would say, "That Sanders girl, or Edna," is just so loose. She is a fass-tale-gal, hot in the britches, and smelling herself. You name it and they called me that! I was called it all, and it bugged me so much. Wait! Let me slow down a bit and talk about why it bugged me.........

I was not bothered that they called me these names because I was still in my (I don't care phase. I didn't care, but I was still a Christian, religious or spiritual person, in the church, whatever you want to call it. I still loved God. I felt that God still cared about me in some kind of way, or something. However, the thing that got me confused was all these church folks! I'm like, so why are y'all holding these titles and long-drawn-out church services talking about *1 Corinthians 12, which discusses the gifts of the spirit:*

The Apostle Paul mentions the following spiritual gifts

1. Word of Wisdom
2. Word of Knowledge
3. Faith
4. Gifts of Healing
5. Working of Miracles
6. Prophecy
7. Discerning of Spirits
8. Various Kinds of Tongues
9. Interpretation of Tongues

What confused me for the longest was why all the other spiritual gifts were working in the church, but no one seemed to have the gift of discerning of spirits. In my list above, it is number seven, discerning of spirits. I honestly still attended church, and I was very active. I would even invite others, win prizes, and get recognized for inviting the most people on numerous occasions. Nonetheless, I was just in awe of how no one ever discerned this foolishness. Yet they could see that I was hot in the tail or fast (however you prefer to say it). but they could not see that it was something beyond the surface happening with me.

I am sure I was screaming for help!

As a matter of fact, I would sometimes sit in my seat during a prophetic service and pray that he would be revealed. I would not call him out myself, no! I didn't want to die. I just wanted someone else to be tough enough to stand up to this giant of a short man in my life.

Sadly, no one stood up!

Every prophetic service was the same, and, tragically, people were saying that God said this and God said that, "yet the majority of it was false, and/or misleading." God doesn't lie, but they made him out to be a liar, and this is how I ended up leaving his home.

THE GREAT ESCAPE

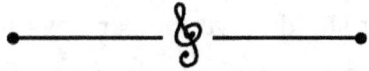

Throughout the many years of growing up in our home, my siblings and I would talk so boldly whenever our parents weren't around. During these times, I would often tell my siblings that I was going to run away. My words would sound so bold and so direct…saying things like, I'm leaving, getting up out of here! Oh, but when I found out that I could leave at age eighteen, my mind was set, and that was my mission. Thankfully, my oldest sister helped me put my plan into action! This was the mission; the great escape, and I believe it came from God because everything connected; all the dots connected for me. We had to strategize a plan for me to be out of the house before my next payday, before my daddy realized that my check wasn't in the mail.

Why, you ask? Well, once again, I'm glad you asked!

Listen, because if I had still been living there, he would've beaten me black and blue for opening a checking account without his permission. My dad would take my work checks. I mean, he would be waiting for that Pactiv check to hit the mail. I had to strategically leave in between pay periods, so this is what I did. I opened a bank account so my check wouldn't go to the house but would be directly deposited into my new bank account. I didn't even have $25 to open my own bank account. I borrowed it from my uncle (His brother) and his wife in Malvern; (whom I am extremely grateful for by the way.) My account was officially opened at the Malvern National Bank, and we (my sister and I) decided that once the family went to revival that night, it would be "The Great Escape!"

The plan was that she'd leave the car keys to the Cadillac, and I could retrieve my things from her car that night. That's exactly what I did! The very same night, I also called the police and told them that I was leaving my parents' home. The police informed me that since I was eighteen, I had the legal right to leave.

I immediately lived with my friend for about two weeks, and then from June to August, I lived with my auntie. (Thanks a million, auntie!) I lived with her until I was enrolled in the Job Corps. I lived at the Little Rock Job Corps Center-dormitories, on 2020 Vance St., and thereafter I moved in with my grandmother, Ercille Divine (My Safe place).

Chapter Three

The Awakening Of My Calling

I love my grandmother, Ercille Devine. This woman is a gem! She doesn't realize how God used her ministry of working with children to lead me to my calling as well. She not only led me into my calling, but she and my mom were a door for me to learn the proper way to nurture, mother with compassion, teach, and interact with children. She was a doorway leading me into liberty and power to learn the proper and effective way to break this generational curse.

As much as I shrugged my shoulders and proclaimed how much I didn't care, she convinced this non-caring young adult to go to college. So, I did understand that college is not for everyone. I was totally against it for the longest, but Children's church is what inspired me to delve deeper into an area where I could become an advocate for voiceless children. So many of the children and youth that I worked with were considered voiceless in my eyes.

IT'S TIME TO EXHALE AND LET IT GO!

Author Edna Sanders

It's just that they weren't allowed to speak up. Parents trusted everyone with their babies. My biggest pet peeve was that parents would believe others about their children, rather than at least listening to their children. I mean, don't get me wrong. I'm a mother now, so I definitely understand a parent knowing their child/children. For example, a teacher could tell me today about my child and an incident that may have occurred... (hand on my head emoji) I am most definitely raising four little sassy Edna-Jr's. (Please say a prayer for me, now, I'm serious) But I try my best to allow them to speak up for themselves, other than just taking someone else's word over my child. I then try to advocate for them, and usually I come to realize that the old saying is right; There are three sides to every story... your side, my side, and the truth. Even now, so many children are being hurt by people who are supposed to protect them with their lives.

While attending my first semester of college at U of A-Pulaski Technical College, in one of my Early Childhood Development courses, I first realized that whippings (especially, in the manner that I received them) were extremely wrong. You should have seen the shock on my face! Although my eyes were open to the fact that my childhood was tougher and rougher than I realized. I did not even know how gory my traumatic experience was until I was learning, studying, and attending more classes about this area.

I mean, yeah, I knew my experience was wrong, nasty, and embarrassing. Yet, I just considered my home situation as well, and at least I made it through. (I sounded so churchy, didn't I?) For the longest, I thought I had buried my emotions about everything, but God has a way of allowing us to see the deeper issues of the heart. He let me see myself through the eyes of another. I graduated from college and began living my life. Even after college, changing church homes, getting married, and having children, I thought that I'd forgiven my father until a new case developed regarding my father.

LOCAL PASTOR ON TRIAL

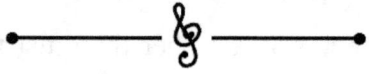

There was so much discussion about my father's trial, and honestly, I had not shared my trauma with anyone. Yet, when this new case developed, and I had the chance to talk to his last victim, all the hate rose up within me all over again. It didn't matter that this new victim was not related to me. With the way I felt, I don't think I could have been any madder if it had been a relative.

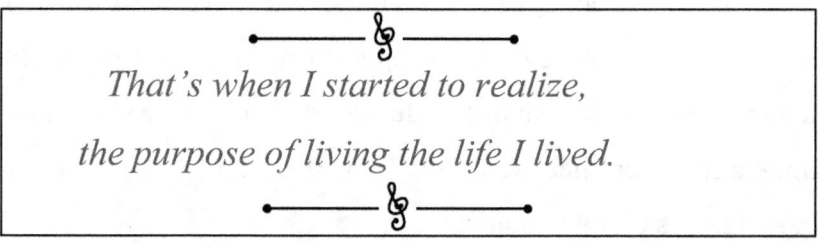
That's when I started to realize,
the purpose of living the life I lived.

Now I didn't quite understand the depth of it all. I just knew I had to change something.... Not quite sure altogether how. but let me tell you; all I knew (please, excuse my French) is that this shit could not happen again, not on my watch! Forgive me, I got off track. Let's get back to our regular scheduled program…

So I talked to his last victim and became so angry. I was honestly angrier with myself because I let him get me this mad again. Y'all don't understand! By this time in my life, I was a wife, a mother, and a devout, sold-out church member, etc.! I was delivered, or so I thought. (In my mind) I thought I had forgiven my dad. I buried my emotions and just didn't think about it. Yet whenever we would go to Malvern or have to go around him, I was extra careful, and I remember saying I forgive you! This case showed me that I had not dealt with everything. I hadn't even seen a therapist, which I should've, but I taught myself to run emotionally.

I skipped out on myself, thinking I was saving myself. I was hoping things would magically heal themselves. The truth is, God needed me to see what was lying dormant in my heart. The little girl in me had been muffled, and while I grew up and accepted this as a part of my life, little Edna was angry and filled with sorrow. Little did I know that little Edna needed to sing her song of pain while soaring into the liberty of love!

During the process of my dad's court case, I became filled with many emotions. I opened myself up to hear from others, but that was draining too. After talking and listening to many people's thoughts and opinions about the case, oh, my goodness. I got so many people's unsolicited thoughts, opinions, and advice. This brought about many emotions at once, a few examples are embarrassment/shame, sadness, regret, panic/frantic, fearfulness, hatred, stress, depression, revenge, anger, and heroism.

I was also called many things by many different people, this list (head shaking emoji, for-real): sell-out, unsaved, hypocrite, Satan, weak, coward, ungrateful, snitch, stupid, bitch, attention whore, liar, (I laugh now at this mess) the good stuff, a protector, a friend, an Esther, a Moses, a leader, and my favorite a helper. The comment that probably got me the most was when someone said… I just wish someone had stood up for me, and that someone was me.

I just wish someone had stood up for me.
and that someone was me.

As I was preparing and getting ready for court, I had to make myself write down every encounter that I remembered about my past. You all, I did not tell y'all everything in this book. Yes, it was graphic just to read the bits and pieces I wrote earlier, but writing it and reliving it for court was agony. I mean, I made myself forget many things. I can't say it enough. I cry now thinking about how I relived everything.

Let me remind you that prior to this case, I'd never openly talked about many of the things that I buried in the back of my mind. I made myself believe that it had never happened when in fact it had happened. As I was saying, while preparing for court, I was debating on backing out of it and just leaving it all alone…. Then, God brought to my remembrance a situation I'd encountered back in high school….

During high school, I enrolled in a group called Project Achievement. This group was an after-school program that did many things with teenagers, such as tutoring, budgeting, college prep, job placements, career readiness training, etc. This one project that God brought to my memory was one where they had us tutoring younger elementary children. Well, during this time, I was about 15 or 16 years old, and one of my students confided in me. I will never forget this day because I was at the READ building helping this little girl. So this particular session, while we were going over her homework. She stopped and looked up at me. She asked, "Can I tell you something?" I was like, yeah, girl what's up (I said her name of course)

THE CONVERSATION
THAT HEAVEN RECORDED

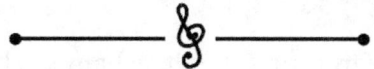

Our conversation went as such:

Child: "I'm scared to go home."

Me: Oh, I was not expecting that, but why are you scared?

Child: "My step daddy is touching me."

Me: What? (I'm frozen as she speaks)

Child: "Yeah, he always touches me down there, and he makes me touch him too. Can you help me? Just don't tell my mommy. She said I am lying."

Me: (crying) I hold her, and we cry together.... I then say I'm so sorry, I really don't know what to do. Can I pray for you? (At that time in my life, it was all I knew to do.)

Child: (crying) She says yes, (so of course, I pray for her)

I wish I could tell you all that...

- I went in there and immediately told the supervisor,
- I would love to tell you that I called the police.
- I wish I could tell you that I called Child Protective Services.
- I even wish I could tell you that I confidently told my mom or some trustworthy adult.

But no; sadly, and regretfully, I felt ashamed. I couldn't tell anyone because I had not shared my own. I was that little girl, even at age fifteen, there I was holding myself, even though I was holding her. I still feel to this day that I let her down. I guess, God's grace helps me by reminding me that I didn't run to help for myself, how could I help someone else? I was going through the same thing that she was going through. Yet this baby was stronger than I.... I hadn't even talked to anyone about what I was going through; not even my own sisters were going through the same thing and sleeping in the same bed as me. She, this baby, this child, had confided in me, and I let her down. I saw her strength and I hate that she used it on a coward.........This is the situation that God instantly brought to my memory during this season of my life. He then presented the question...

Now, what are you going to do?

One of my go-to core values (if that's what you want to call it) is: When you know better, do better. This baby girl's strength was an avenue to provoke or encourage me to break this generational curse. So yes, I let this situation with this younger child help boost my confidence to help this older child with her situation. It just so happened that the older girl's situation involved the same person who caused much of my emotional and physical pain.

My dad....

I will stop here briefly to say that if you're ever in a situation as such...
This is a resource to get the child the help they may need.
The Arkansas Child Abuse Hotline Phone number is:

1-844-SAVE-A-CHILD, or 1-800-482-59

Even after the case, people would ask questions such as, Edna, "If you were so hurt by your dad as you say, then why still go to church?" I knew the evil intent behind that question because people can only see through the lens of their opinions and not the realities of a little girl being raped. I was a child, so I couldn't leave, nor could I make my own decisions. I did what I thought a good little girl was supposed to do, but I must admit now that I'm older, some of those scriptures stuck with me. The scriptures (real word of God) were taking root in me, and I didn't know it. I needed to see God for myself and his love for me.

See this same man who did so many unthinkable things to me had me do unthinkable things to him and taught all six of his children to read God's word for ourselves. He would preach consistently about how important it was to have our relationship with God, and somewhere in this journey, trying to maintain a (religious) relationship with God was my main goal. My relationship with God is the only reason I can say this. My love for what Jesus did for me on the cross is why I don't hold hate in my heart for my dad. God's patience with me in my (I don't care days led me into being a caring person. God changed my heart.

Let me explain (a little bit)

Once I graduated from high school, I decided that I wanted to be celibate. I wanted God to transform me like he did those people I read about in the Bible. I wanted God to show me that the Bible was not wrong. I would think to myself, Lord, please let something be real about this Bible, they forced me to learn, all these years. My goodness! I just wanted to see for myself how real God is. I did not want to continue to be a hypocrite. I did not like walking around angry all the time. I enjoyed being friendly! Let me remind you, I am a hugger, and nobody wants a grouchy-looking hugger hugging them. Laughing to myself,

I told myself that I could not afford to walk around hating my dad and my past anymore. I will tell you forgiveness is a process, and it was even harder when he'd give me biblical scripture to show and tell me that what we did or were doing was a sin. My siblings and I just obeyed him because we were afraid of him. I say we because, like I said earlier, it is six of us siblings. We were all afraid in our own way. So much so that one of my sisters and I were going through similar experiences in the same house, sometimes even during the same day or night, and we honestly never spoke of it to each other until years later. We were both married with our own families before we even talked to each other about the sexual things that happened to us while growing up in the place we called home.

My Letter To My Dad

Dear Daddy,

I am having a hard time starting this letter to you. How weird is that? I'm super emotional, but I promised little Edna that I'd release her last song. So here goes...

Daddy, I forgive you. I honestly, from my heart, forgive you.

I have heard so many people say the saying that hurt people, hurt people, and it could be true in your case (I don't doubt it). I can't imagine the hurt you may have hidden in your heart. I hate to think of who may have hurt you or what situation triggered you to inflict hurt on us.

Daddy, I loved you………I do love you.

It used to make me so annoyed when I would tell you that I love you and you say things like "I can't tell since you got me in here"…. Or I can't tell you're not giving me any money or jumping when you say jump. (Something along those lines) I didn't realize how much emotional pain this situation caused. I think the emotional and spiritual aspects became worse than the physical act alone. One example of how the emotional and spiritual became worse is that I found myself trying to prove my love to people by spending money on them. I didn't think people cared or accepted that I honestly loved them if I wasn't spending money on them or if I wasn't breaking myself physically to be there. I was broken and empty. I am saying this only to inform you of what I am fighting; and to let you know that it is not the only way to show people that you love them. I hope you *are healing, Daddy. I hope you are stronger, and I wish you well. I want only God's blessings for you. My children only know bits and pieces of their papaw, and I'm okay with that. I will answer their questions about you. But look, see, daddy, I recall how you would say often in your sermons. "I'm a scriptural preacher!" I know your method of communication very well, so follow me to the book of Proverbs.*

Proverbs 4:23 KJV reads as such.

"Keep thy heart with all diligence; for out of it are the issues of life."

Well, this says to me, (in this time I've had to heal...) Edna, your first and most important ministry is home, which includes: ME (God with-in) + my spouse (when I have him) + my children = MY HEART!

Daddy, I am guarding my heart, and this peace I have (that surpasses all understanding). Remember, Dad, you told me about that Peace. I pray you truly get that Peace. I am guarding my heart, and all it consists of, diligently and consistently. Yes, they will know the good and decent things about you, and my upbringing. They will also know the not-so-good because there is some truth to that Bible. I trust that we will be able to (positively and peacefully) manage the issues of life. I just cannot continue to force myself to prove to you or anyone else that I love them. As I conclude, I cannot grow if I continue to hate or blame you for all my flaws. Spending money to prove my love is one of the kinks that I'm going to have to work out on my own. I'll make it, you hear me, daddy, and I'll keep singing songs of healing.

But daddy, I don't want you to get weary in well doing.

You did do some good things, and we laugh about them often in our sibling group chat. You taught us to believe in God, and for that I am forever grateful. There is so much greatness in you. You raised some wonderful children. We are all respectful (to an extent). Thank you for all the wonderful meals and trips. Man, I still don't know how we were able to travel around the United States summer after summer with six children! I am trying to plan trips for me and my six. Needless to say, I get overwhelmed. You took us all around, up, down, left, and right. We cannot go anywhere to this day without someone saying, "Hey, aren't you a Sanders? Y'all sang at our church years ago." You taught us the importance of family, and we are always there for each other. Yes, we fought, but we got it right because we knew Daddy did not play that.

We are respectful to everyone because of your teaching. Thank you. I will not blame you for my flaws, especially now that I am grown.. I know better, and it's time for me to do better.

I forgive you, and I love you.

Sincerely, Edna Sanders

Part Two

Overcoming The Present

Enough is enough! I'm still forgiving myself and others.

Chapter Four

Masquerading behind a Toxic Love and an (Un)healed Life

When I first began this journey of writing my book, I didn't know how to include this section, in being that I was living in my divorce season while trying to peacefully co-parent; it felt like life was creating its own mental barrier. Writer's block hit hard here. I admit I was still healing through the layers; I wasn't quite ready to speak about it all. Even now, I am living this situation (present-day). I still have to remain mindful of the fact that we have children.

Our children can read, and I refuse to speak negatively about their dad in their presence, and I will try to avoid it as much as possible in this book because my book shares so many truths about myself. I will share a few short stories and an assortment of journal entries I wrote to myself.

I am big on people taking accountability…so, yes, I will start there…I used to hear people say this often... "You made the bed; you've got to lay in it" …. I took it to mean Look, you know what you signed up for, so handle it…. This was my mindset in this phase of my life… It was a very long season yet I learned so much about myself and how my past traumas aided in my being oblivious to many red flag moments and toxic situations. Choosing not to heal before marriage opened me up to more toxicity. I was a broken girl already who assumed she'd healed from an unseen amount of abuse. I associated healing with being involved with my church, attending multiple church services, joining/leading various departments within the church, racing to many altar calls, being a part of many groups, obtaining higher positions within my career, and fulfilling all of my motherly and wifely duties.

I guess I assumed that because I was married, all of the past would magically disappear, and Edna would have her happily ever after. I mean, why would that not be right? Yeah, I sinned, but Jesus is gracious! I asked for forgiveness and now look! (Isn't that how it works, right?) I mean, I really started making a mental list of the good things I was doing:

- I am married. I don't ever cheat, I cook, clean, run errands, fulfill my wifely obligations, and I'm not a brawling woman. I apologized as soon as I felt I'd overstepped when talking to him! I taught him this., I taught him that. (I'm a good wife!)
- I was married when I got pregnant with all my children, and they all have the same daddy! (I would normally smile big on this one) (literally, rolling eyes emoji now)
- I work. I don't steal, I pay the bills even when he's not working, I pay them even when he just doesn't feel like paying them… I do it! (I needed some help, literally and figuratively)

- I am meek, I am chaste, I fast, I pray, I give to everyone, and I overgive!
- I follow the J.O.Y acronym to a "T"! They would teach us that if you want Joy in life, you have to put Jesus first, Others next, and Yourself last.
- I go to church regularly, and beyond that. I was at most every service, and I wasn't forced to do so like I was as a child. (So, I'm really earning some brownie points, God!)

I mean, this list was horribly long and filled with so many self-righteous ideologies. I needed: a reality check, life coaching, therapy, and some major self-reflections. Sadly I entered into this wife phase of life based solely on a little bit of a college education, a heaping helping of lustful emotions, a desire to be nothing like my dad, except for church, and God (I definitely still wanted what I knew to be a relationship with God) and last but not least, I had a lot of faith that he'd (my ex-husband) protect me from my past. I handed my broken fragments of a life over to a very young man who needed healing himself. The more I reveal the hurt I buried, the more my journey becomes clearer. I've written this section from my diary because even when I wasn't pursuing healing, healing was pursuing me by prompting me to write.

I wrote a few late-night messages in my diary before I filed for divorce. In all honesty, I had forgotten about these journal entries. Then one night, during the process of getting this book published, I stumbled upon my notes app. I don't know about you, but I love to read old diary submissions and old prayer requests, and as I read through, I see how God has answered many of my silent prayers. Strolling through my past diary submissions, I see myself then, and my mindset now. Uhm, all I can say is it's a God thing. I realize that I was already second-guessing us and myself before the divorce. How did I keep this going for fifteen years? Is a question to truly be asked? This means I convinced myself to remain in something that was destroying me. I had the courage to leave my father's house when I was eighteen, "but not enough courage and/or confidence to leave a debilitating and stagnant relationship."

IS IT REALLY WORTH IT

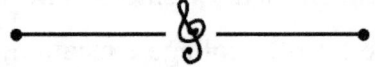

JANUARY 19, 2020 – DIARY OF EDNA SANDERS

I'm so emotional right now. Well maybe I am about to start my cycle! I'm so annoyed with my husband and myself. I'm mad at myself because I don't know what choices to make concerning myself, my children, and my husband. It's like I'm married, but doing everything all alone!

- Isn't he supposed to be our leader?
- Shouldn't I be able to ask him and find help from him?

God, I don't know. How can you put their lives in my hands? I'm so inconsistent! I'm so undisciplined. I am slow to understand, too anxious, and so defensive.

Did I forget to mention that I am too emotional? I just don't understand how or why we're chosen to take care of Patrick and little Daniel... not just them, even these girls: Braisly, Kinslee Charity, and Trinity. I don't want to fail them, I don't want to fail my husband. I don't want to fail you, God, and I don't want to fail myself. I just feel like I succeed at nothing.

- Yes, I guess I can sing
- I can help,
- I can do various other things when I work at it.

Honestly, I think I've lost my desire to work and serve. I've been working for so long, and now when I take a break, stop to rest, or plainly just do nothing, then people (especially my husband) make like I haven't done anything? I'm tired, lost, confused, and drained. I can't even help myself, how can I help someone else?

I'M BETTER TODAY

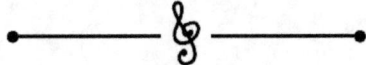

January 20, 2020 – Diary Of Edna Sanders

So, it is now Tuesday, and I just thought about how my husband woke me to go check on our daughter, who was sleeping, but she wasn't asleep. Trinity was whining and scratching her legs. I was asking questions but not getting any answers. I then assumed that something must be biting her or something, so I intended to find her some cream, lotion, or something. However, when I got out of bed, I realized that I needed to potty. While doing this, Trinity started crying a bit louder. She then found her way into the bathroom, holding her ear. I said, "Trinity, what is wrong is your ear hurting?"

She said yes. I immediately started searching for pain meds. I treated the main problem first, gave her a Kleenex to put in her ear, then after that, I was led to rub lotion mixed with peppermint oil on her leg. Finally, Trinity and my husband are both sleeping soundly. This was a victory for me. I had honest joy in my heart because I helped my baby feel better and helped my husband sleep better. The other day, I was feeling overwhelmed and overworked. I'm learning that I need to change my perception.

I am a natural-born helper because I was so pleased just to know that my baby was not hurting as much anymore. I was happy knowing that my baby could rest if only for a little while. I was happy knowing that my baby girl and my husband knew who to call on naturally when they needed help, and happy knowing that I was there, and I was not upset about working/serving.

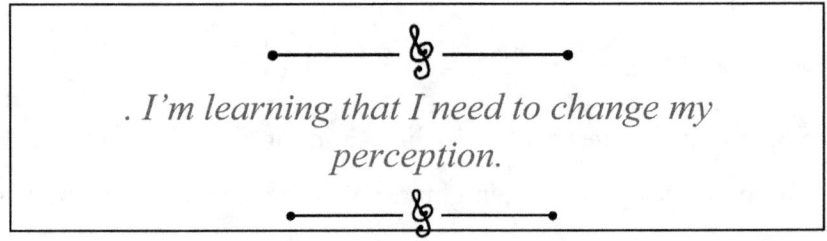

. I'm learning that I need to change my perception.

God, I know that you woke me up tonight to tell me to change my perspective regarding helping people. I am to help from a pure motive, without looking for something in return. I'm so glad that I feel better. God has a way of doing things and I like the way that he does it! Lord, help me to help with a grateful heart.

COUNTING OUR WINS

January 20th -28th, 2020 – Diary Of Edna Sanders

Thursday, Jan. 20

God woke me up! We met my boy's biological sister, and I helped my church plan for Sunday school.

Friday, Jan.21

God woke me up! I was able to talk to my mother-in-law about my marriage, and she helped me. I really felt better after talking with her. (Sad but good) I spoke with my oldest daughter about her birthday, and I would have to push back her celebration or do something less expensive due to financial reasons. She said, "Mommy, it's okay, you don't have to do anything; It's okay. I know you still love me." My mommy asked to keep the children for the entire weekend, and my husband drove them to Malvern. I was able to complete all my homework assignments for the week!

Saturday, Jan 22

God woke me up! I didn't have any homework today. I was able to attend my coworker's mother's funeral, and my husband and I had a wonderful date today. We got our nails done, went to a restaurant for brunch, and we took a nap! Hallelujah! We later joined our virtual Sunday school classes! We went to a local family choir rehearsal and after I tried to look up a little bit of information about overcoming.

Sunday, Jan. 23

God woke me up! Church was awesome. "Blessed with a limp" was the subject. My husband and I found a different route to Malvern. We were lost, annoyed, and aggravated with each other during the process, but we rejoiced when we saw familiar areas. We made it to our destination without (much) arguing or without turning around. He preached, and souls were blessed and encouraged! We came back to Jacksonville and fellowshipped with our families!

Mon. Jan. 24

God woke me up, and I folded up some clothes.

Tues. Jan. 25

God woke me up! I am able to quarantine and get paid for it. One child out of 6 tested positive, but she is feeling good.

Wed. Jan. 26

God woke me up, and I did a lot of schoolwork online.

Thurs. Jan. 27

God woke me up! Today is my Braisly's birthday!! 11 years! I made her a cake, and I was able to get her two gifts, and she was happy. Mary surprised me and came by the house!

Fri. Jan. 28

God woke me up!! I made a plan for our finances. We were married for thirteen years. Although we were together for fifteen years, now we are headed for a divorce.

SO CONFUSED, WHAT DO I DO

September – December 2021 – Diary Of Edna Sanders

Am I really this desperate or broken, to be with this man, that I ignore him boldly and carelessly, cheating on me in my face... I was helping him clean his wounds and change his bandages when I noticed him texting other women. This would happen whenever I would step away. He would act sleepy as long as I was in the room, then as soon as I stepped away, into the restroom or in the hallway to talk to a nurse or get supplies of some kind, he'd muster up enough strength to text and call his women. I recall him asking one of those ladies to send him pictures of her while he was lying in the hospital bed. Yeah, I was totally lost, confused or just purposely ignoring his actions. I probably should have left him there to fend for himself... but no, I didn't I just kept on helping him and eventually cried about it later... Here's my 2 a.m. thoughts on this situation and how broken and incomplete I felt in this season.

Okay, so what is really going on? I'm like nothing is going on right now! Lord, what are you teaching me? What do you want me to learn from these ongoing situations and trials? I'm so over crying right now. I just don't know what to do. I know the Bible mentioned how Paul said that every time I try to do good evil is always present with me. Yet some things I'm going through I don't know if it's evil, self-initiated, or a test of some sort? How do I learn the difference? How do we grow from this? I'm just so confused. What do I do? I'm like really sad. Here's a list of some things that have been causing me confusion: my credit was growing; I was paying off things and using less credit.... Now two of my 3 credit cards are almost maxed out. My credit score is dropping!!!-My bills were getting paid on time!!! Now I have to get extensions. I had money to bless people/others, I was able to be a lender, not a borrower (like your word says), but now I'm doing all I can not to ask for help from others. My body has been feeling weak lately, even though I don't talk about it. I don't want to seem weak, not only that, I'm the only person working in our home.

We don't qualify for food stamps (hallelujah) but we have been getting the P-EBT SNAP benefits (hallelujah) My children bring me up and down I just seem to never stop having to fix things when it comes to them. Something is always lost or broken and mom is the only solution to the problem. My husband is doing the most lately, a whole-nother headache himself! I worry if I'm a good wife/friend, I want to help him, but I get frustrated because he doesn't seem to hear my silent and loud screams for help. I'm broken on the inside. Why do I have to give in all of the time? My weight was coming off then I wasn't disciplined enough to maintain it. Although my husband would bring fattening food around me all the time! Now he's losing weight praise God and congratulations but I'm sad that he didn't try to help me keep a healthy lifestyle. (I know that's jealousy and no accountability on my part.) I pray I get that out of me, but why didn't he try to help me like I helped him? Yes, I bring unhealthy food around him sometimes but not consistently like he used to do me. Yet I don't know. I just don't think he cares much for me anymore, anyway. That's my thing, I am tired of caring about what people think of me, yet I still get hurt when I even feel like they think something negative about me, especially with my husband. I wish I didn't care so much.

STILL CONFUSED, WHAT DO I DO

April 30th, 2022 – Diary Of Edna Sanders

I'm sure I don't understand everything you do and think about, but I'm definitely not worth being treated like I'm worth nothing to you. We're not perfect, you or I, but we should both respect each other. I should not have to wonder if my husband thinks I'm beautiful, or cute, etc. I do want you so bad, but I'm not going to beg you to want me. It is not okay to ask me for gas money for work, etc., and you sit in the car wasting gasoline, smoking every night.

How do you think it's okay to buy weed every week but not fully pay your portion of the bills? I'm not wrong for mentioning this to you. We're supposed to work together, but you love letting others pick up the slack. His thing is to do as little as possible so someone else can come fix the mess or pay for it. Especially his Edna. She gets so much money a month (No, he doesn't know or care to know what all she does with the money, with a household of 8, What am I doing? Niggah! I'm keeping a roof over our head with no help from you. You are dead weight!) I want a divorce. I can't do this anymore!

FILED FOR DIVORCE

June 22nd, 2022 - Diary Of Edna Sanders

Wow! Really, how is this it? How did it get this far? Why did I allow myself to wait fifteen years before I realized I needed to end this relationship? Why didn't I act when I saw the signs years ago? How will I move forward? What will my children think of me? Will they hate me? Will they still love me? Do they love me? Will anyone ever love me? Did he even truly love me? How did I let myself down like this? How did I stop caring for myself? Why don't I love myself like I need to? How can

I love myself? Did I do my best? Could I have done more? Could I have been better?

These are the questions I am currently asking myself. I am asking God; I am asking anyone who will listen. I am really feeling blind. I feel like I'm walking lost. I feel like I have no vision. I feel like my life is just wandering aimlessly. Although somewhere deep within me I feel a sense of hope. Yes, I feel lost, but I don't feel alone. I sense a presence near me. Yes, fear tries to override and make me fearful with anxiety. This presence is the presence I have felt with me throughout my entire life. I felt this presence when I left my parents' home in the summer of 2004. The only way I can express it is that I felt a sense of nervousness, yet I felt like I had to do it. I was unsure what the result would bring about, but I knew I had to get away. I also felt this same feeling when I moved to Job Corps soon after, and I was definitely unsure of what to expect.

I was fearful, but I felt like I had to go to a different place. I can say that I was thankful for the experiences and the people I met during those transitions. I was also able to be used in various ways to introduce people to Christ and minister through my service to them in some kind of way. I am saying that God's presence was with me during those times. God had a plan for me even during those times. I can't sit here and say I made the right decisions concerning my life. However, I can say that in my unsure decision-making process, God has always been with me, even after those times. I am currently almost a month in since I filed for divorce from my husband of thirteen years.

We have four biological children (daughters), and two boys we adopted (sons). We have grown apart. I am just shocked that I did it. I am sad only because I never wanted to hurt anyone, especially Him! No, not my husband, I loved him with everything in me. I even love him now yet I will leave him a hundred times rather than cause him any more pain. I will stay away from him forever if being around me makes his skin crawl. He may say that's not the case, but that's exactly how he acted these last two years whenever he came home. He didn't want to be here so I freed him from me. I am aware that life is happening. I am aware that I did not do everything right in our marriage. I realize that some people are in our lives for a season. This is not the situation. Fortunately, my ex-husband and I have six wonderful children and therefore we will be in each other's lives forever. Yet we have grown apart and it's okay. There are many things I am thankful for my ex-husband. I have come to realize that I want to grow. I know this divorce is still recent in my life, yet I can't grow if I continue to carry hate or anger towards him.

THE EMOTIONAL DIVORCE

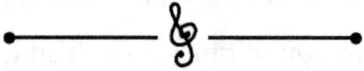

As you continue to read this book, you will see that I bring in songs that have helped me. You will also realize how (uniquely me, I am. In this season of my life, I have so many songs ministering to me in various ways. Although I actually could not find a song (initially) to help me through this divorce. I say to myself many things, such as:

How can I write about crying my last tear, ***"Yesterday" (by Mary, Mary)***, and I'm crying right now? How can I write about ***"Accept What God Allows"* (by *Richard White and Twinkie Clark*)**, and I'm not sure if it's God or me? How can I sing ***"I Am What God Says I Am" (by Bishop Jeff Banks & Revival Temple Community Choir)***, and I seem to be failing at life right now?

Honestly, the main songs ringing loud in my ear (in this moment) are not holy; for example, ***"Bust your Windows"* by Jazmine Sullivan** is ringing super-duper loud!

- I am hurt and sad
- I am embarrassed and annoyed!
- I am tired and angry!

We were married for thirteen years. Although we were together for fifteen years. Yes, I understand that people have been married longer than us, but it doesn't make it hurt any less. I entered this union on March 6, 2010. We have six children together. During my childbearing days, he was excellent during labor, delivery, and caring for us when we came home from the hospital. He helped me bring four beautiful daughters into this world. He then stood up like the leader I always hoped for him to be when he agreed to adopt our two boys. He was most definitely the man I needed during the past season of my life. He was the man who I thought I needed to stand up to my giant of a dad. I will never forget him for that. But seriously, I walked into this marriage hopeful and optimistic. I walked in thinking that we could work out any situation. I'm thinking that I will have a forever best friend. protector, provider, prayer partner, a lifetime of love making, and a leader for our family. I assumed that I was everything he needed and wanted. I assumed that I was a submissive wife; I was striving to be the Proverbs 31 woman.

Ya'll know that woman. Proverbs 31:10-31 KJV

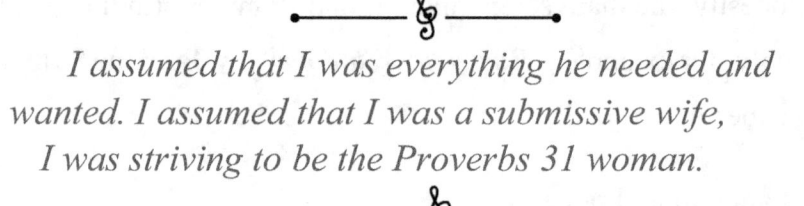

I assumed that I was everything he needed and wanted. I assumed that I was a submissive wife, I was striving to be the Proverbs 31 woman.

I assumed that we were content with each other. However, throughout our marriage, I began to assume that this was a normal marriage. I had just decided that okay, yeah, we're having ups and downs, yes, we're arguing a lot. but this is normal! We will eventually make up and grow past this. I then realized we were yelling nonstop and getting extremely annoyed whenever we would come around each other. I would always hold down a job and pick up the slack while he had options to pay the bills or not. Then we'd fake it for family, friends, church or public functions so it seemed like we had a happy marriage.

The irony is we'd make up and everything just to go through the motions so that our lie seemed more real while we knew we were faking. Once we'd get back home, we would start back arguing. We seemed to put on so much that many people would call us a power couple. Here I am living another lie for the faces of people while internally struggling. People pleasing had overtaken me, and I was fed up with living the lies.

There's a back story to all of this, and I'm ready to share it.

But what sealed the deal for me was when this man stood up to my dad.

Upon dating my former husband, I had never, I mean ever been in a relationship before, so he was my first real relationship. I was not allowed to date, and so my only hookups before marriage were what y'all call sneaky links these days.

So… when I finally got into an official boyfriend/girlfriend relationship, we were doing the thang consistently, I guess I decided to be saved for a second and say that we can't be hypocrites, being that I was over the youth department and all that jazz. We were both in agreement that we believed in marriage.

Rant begins… Listen, I am a person who stands up for the underdog. So, if someone is getting picked on, I don't mind intervening. However, for some reason, I had never seen anyone stand up for me. (siblings, friends, cousins, etc.) One of my siblings said, "I didn't think that you needed any help because you were always so tough. You would fight the people that bothered us, so we assumed that you were ok." People listen! Your strong friends or siblings need to know that you have them, too. I can't stress it enough! Just because we seem strong on the outside does not mean that we don't quiver on the inside or that we can handle every situation alone. My goodness, how come it's not common knowledge to help the person who helps you? It should be automatic, right? Well, it's not. **Rant over...**

He stood up to my father, and I was so appreciative of someone standing up for me that I strongly felt that he was the one. Our marriage happened because two protectors bonded, but the problem was that we weren't healed of our own trauma while trying to protect each other from the past. He had battles that he overcame, and so did I. I can now say that my marriage was based on a lot of assumptions that never became a reality for us. The only reality was divorce. It may be hard to believe, but my purpose for this project is not to destroy anyone. It's just a testament to God's guiding hand in my life.

I say that because I am healed enough now to know that the many choices I made in life were not the best, and many of my adult decisions were made from the mind of a trauma-filled, unhealed young adult. I can't state how important it is to heal, heal, heal! Work on yourself before you decide to get into a relationship with anyone. In retrospect, I see that many times I should have just stepped aside and pressed reset on my life. I should have done that before engaging with another unhealed person (anyone, for that matter). You could probably say we were a modern-day visual of the blind leading the blind.

My Letter to My Ex-Husband

Dear Former Husband,

    Well, this is emotional for me, but it must be done. This is me realizing that we're finished. Yes, yes, I know we are stuck like Chuck because of the children. Yet, we are not each other's everything, and I totally get it. Wow, fifteen years of marriage!

Laugh to keep from crying

I know you will read this book and see all of my comical comments about being relieved and whatnot, yet you also know that I like to play. You also know that many times I laugh to keep from crying (as we both do). Anyway, my goal in this letter is for two things: 1) Let you know that I forgive you, and 2) Thank you. I forgive you for everything. I don't hate you and I never will. (Yes, I really dislike your words and some of your ways, but not you as a person)

Learned a lot together

I want to thank you because I have learned a lot from you. We have learned a lot together. Thank you so much for showing me that I can trust you with our daughters. Thank you (as I am wiping tears from my eyes) for helping me through all our pregnancies and being there for everyone. Thank you for encouraging me to sing and come out of my shell. I honestly don't think I even would have stepped out as much as I did if you had not pushed me. Thank you for agreeing to be the daddy to our two sons. Thank you for encouraging me, and for being that person (for that season)

Living from the healed version of me

I am finding out a lot about myself. I am aware that I could have done many things differently in our marriage. Yet, I know for a fact, that I was a great wife to you. I have gone back and forth about even mentioning anything positive about myself. For you know that I have always been one to downplay my good qualities and encourage others. However, I will not downplay how good of a wife, friend, mother, or person I am to you and/or anyone anymore. I have never entertained another man (ever) in our marriage. My only focus and priority was you, our family, and our religion/church life. I went above and beyond for you and them to the point where I started slowly killing myself physically and mentally by not setting boundaries to focus on healing. We both needed to heal and learn ourselves before we embarked on this journey, but hey, should-a/could-a/would-a…… We'll be better from here on out.

Loving myself enough to let go

As I conclude, I must say that due to our miscommunication during these last couple of years together, I'm still confused as to why you say (you hate that you ever met me). However, I will not stress myself anymore wondering what I could have done better. I give that back to you. I did enough. I will not say that I did my best. However, I will say that I did too much, in that season, for that season. But my best is yet to come. I have so much more to offer, and I'm saving the best for me. My intent/motive was never to hurt you, never. I only tried to help you and love you. I tried to be your helpmate, and I was… until I couldn't anymore. In the words of a dear friend, may God bless you on your journey.

Sincerely, **Edna Sanders, The healed version**

Chapter Five

Self-Discovery Through My Parenting Style

This marriage taught me to have unconditional love. I learned that I could love someone more than I loved myself, and more than the love that was shown to me. Even though I admit this, I don't like it. I had to unlearn so much as I learned how to love myself. I can't quote the exact person because I have heard so many people say this saying. "How can you pour from an empty pitcher?"

I found myself giving my heart reminders like, Edna take care of yourself, otherwise you won't be able to take care of him or them (my children). The truth is, I just wanted Him to want it for me. I wanted him to see the fact that I was working endlessly for our family and to cherish me and notice my hard work. At least let me know that you don't plan for this to be a continuous cycle. I didn't mind doing anything for him and our family. Just don't make me feel like I'm "The Help." Reassure me that this was only for a season. I wanted help, Dam-A- break!

Journey of An Overcomer

GATHERING THE PIECES OF MY LIFE

Author Edna Sanders

I wanted a tag team, a partner, but hey, should-a, could-a, would-a…it's over now…I am challenging my current self to take advantage of opportunities to do things for Edna.

Although during this season, I've had moments of sadness. "I'm sure you all will call it depression or anxiety. When I seem to hit a road bump and then another, and another, I tend to get really down on myself. I started second-guessing my parenting skills when I know that's one of my best qualities yet! These thoughts came to me because of various life situations, such as:

- I didn't make all their appointments on time
- I bought fast food versus cooking,
- Going to court with my daughters because of bullying
- Did she learn it from her dad and me fighting?
- Did I let another generational curse sneak in?
- How am I teaching them not to hit when that's my only form of discipline?
- Edna, you are not even disciplined yourself, how can you teach your children?
- I almost had to hang my six- and seven-year-olds by the toes (lol)
- I can't get my 4-year-old to speak up, and out,
- My 3-year-old and this potty training is a struggle, when I am handling it like a champ at work!
- And then this gentle parenting has its ups and downs!

PARENTING THROUGH THE DIVORCE

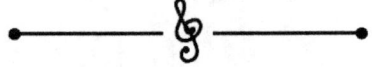

    Throughout all of this, year in and year out, I found myself mostly concerned about our children. I was concerned about how they saw us. I was concerned about their thoughts of me as their mom.

Here is a list of my inward thoughts (concerning my children) during this time: I wondered how our children really feel about us/me.

- Do they see me as a weak mom?
- Do they think I'm a coward?
- Do they feel like I only yell at them and spank them?
- Do they act like they love me on the outside but inwardly hate me?
- Am I a role model for my own children?
- Are they laughing at me?
- Are they using me as a doormat, too?
- Do they think I am a hypocrite?
- Are my children afraid of me?
- Do they trust me?
- Will they talk to me if they are hurt?
- Will they stay away from me vs. reach out to me when they need anything?
- Is my home safe for my own children?

So many crazy thoughts have been going on in this mom brain of mine. I kept thinking things like:

- Will they leave if I'm not being everything for them?
- Will I ever be enough for them?
- Will I have to pay Child support?
- Will I have to pay alimony?
- Will I budget correctly?
- Will I fail my children?
- Will I ever be enough for anyone?
- Will this rose be my partner for the rest of my life????
- Ya'll, the questions are coming!

First of all, I know I am an overthinker. I am that person overthinking everything! I am working on this weakness. I just thought these things, because at some point in my life, I thought like this about my own mom. I hate to say it… I had moments in my childhood when I did not understand why my mom stayed in her marriage. (I may be totally out of order, and if I am, then I'm sorry, Mom)

I recall moments where I would pray and wish for Momma to sneak into the room and show some strength like my girl Tina Turner did in the movie "What's Love Got To Do With It." I watched it as a teenager, and I remember when Tina gathered up her children to leave him. She caught that bus and had almost made it the first time. Ya'll, I was so mad when she had to get off that bus!

OMG! Ok, Ok. I know once again I have gotten sidetracked, but during that season in my life, that movie was a visual of what I hoped would happen. I know Tina did not come out of the abuse in that very moment, however, she eventually left the abuse that was destroying her. I just wanted that. I wanted to see that strength as a child in our home.

Although now as an adult, a mom, ex-wife, and future wife, I see a form of strength in my mom's devotion. I see strength in her faith. I see strength in her loyalty to her commitments. She was committed to her husband, her children, her job, and her goals, and definitely to her God. She is the epitome of strength.

DO YOU NOTICE MY FRUIT?

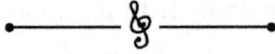

I believe that since I am a believer. I should show some fruit of the Spirit somewhere. My children, who see me every day, should be able to notice my fruit everywhere, such as at home, at church, school, work, the store, and anywhere I go. I should not be different at home than I am everywhere else, and I am talking about Edna, me.... I felt the difference as I made the decisions I made, and I did not want to tarnish their thinking. I had already done enough. My inward fear is being a replica of my dad. (not because of hate) but more so because he seemed to allow his desires to override the highest power within him (which was supposed to be God's power).

I know I have the power of God inside of me. I know I can hear God telling me many things when I am parenting my children. The Holy Ghost speaks loud and clear (sometimes) (some may call it your inner self, or common knowledge, either way, please LISTEN!! I hear the Holy Spirit a lot more when I am disciplining my children.

A few examples are:

Edna, stop yelling. talk calmly.

Edna, that is enough.

Edna, go sit down, don't spank them this way, or in that way, and so many more ways. I want to continue to hear God's voice as I raise my children or anyone's child. I don't want to turn a deaf ear to God. Before I filed for divorce. I started to feel the way that I felt while I was growing up in my father's and mother's home. I just can't.... I can't be fake!

I am raising children who won't have to recover from me raising them, before they can develop into the people God created them to be. I had to recover from the way I was raised. Yes, I know our life situations is what grow us and make us, I know. However, I don't want to be the cause of their pain. I just don't want to offend God's little ones. It matters to God how we treat our children! I want to be like my mom in the sense of loving my children unconditionally,

I recall being in the Job Corps in my early adulthood, and I would receive a letter in the mail from my precious mom. This doll would see me on Sunday, Tuesday, and Friday, unless it was a revival, then it would be every night for church. Yet she would have a letter in her Bible for me, and I would still have a letter in the mail at Job Corps that same week. I don't know how she had time to sit and write two or more letters a week to encourage me, while still handling all her other obligations; and trust me, she had a ton of them. Yet she wanted to remind me that God doesn't just care for me.

She'd say, "No daughter, he continues to care for you even when you think he can't care anymore. Even when you think your load is too heavy for you, yes, it is too heavy for you and me, that's why he wants us to continue to trust the God of our salvation. God is in us to help us with every load, no matter how big or how light it may be. Trust God enough to cast all your cares on him. I love to hear my mom sing." *"Carry your Burdens to the Lord and leave them there."*

My Letter To My Mom

Dear Mom,

I love you. You are my girl. Momma, I have always looked up to you. I have always admired your work ethic. As I study you, I find out that you are rare. I found out I could not have been more blessed.

Momma, I love your commitment

Momma, you stayed when you could have left. I wish I had the eloquent words and scriptures to match my thoughts that define you to me. But momma!!!! You are so much more than those words. I see your strength and I admire it. I must apologize to you. I apologize for my past thoughts, and for letting you down about the divorce, but you have a different strength than me.

I have a different sense or idea of loyalty. I do love you for your strength and loyalty. I love you for you but I realize what's best for me and my heart. I thank you for helping me with this transitional phase in my life. I have probably been home more in the last year than in my entire fifteen-year marriage. The song we sing in the church comes to my mind, something like.. "throw out the lifeline, for someone is drifting away, or someone is sinking today, (however it goes). Momma, I was drifting and sinking, and I saw your lifeline. You saw greatness in me many years ago. I was recently telling my friend how I remember you getting tired of getting phone calls from the school about me. This one particular morning Momma woke all of us up for school, but me, well, the belt woke me up. Momma you beat my butt from when I got out the bed, to using the bathroom, brushing my teeth, putting on my clothes, and running out the front door!

I laugh now, about it but you were talking to me at the same time you were beating my butt. You would ask me, Who's the Smartest person in your class? Who's the best-behaved person in your class? And me being clueless and trying to dodge the hits, I'm calling out the various students' names in my class. Well, you didn't like those answers. Mom, you said no, it's Edna! Say Edna is the best-behaved student, and Edna is the smartest. etc.

I do remember the teacher telling me that you called to see how Edna was doing that day, and let's just say, you got the job done. I had a great day that day. Although that was funny it worked. I also see how you mothered us in your own way as we needed it. You are firm when you needed to be and most definitely were soft and nurturing when needed. I love the gentle hugs, and I needed the church pinches in its own timing. Every now and then I probably could still use a church pinch. Thank you for showing me what I needed to see to be the mom I need to be for this time in my life.

Momma, you have been an anchor for me.

After sharing about how disciplined you were, I have to discuss your slick/comical/and sarcastic side. I am reminded of this time; you may not remember, but you may. There was this one time when my ex-husband and I were shacking up and you came to me one day and said Edna, I'm going on a fast until y'all stop shacking. I was like no ma'am, momma, please don't do that! I don't want you to do that, please! So of course, I continued to stay with my fiancé and I forgot about it but, momma, you know you fasted until I came out of that sin. Do you remember reminding me of it a few weeks before my wedding? After church one night, you hugged me so tight and said Edna, my daughter, my baby... I love you, but I had to start eating!

I was like, what, wait? Why have you not been eating? Are you sick? You with your ever so clever self, say well, you know I was fasting for you all to stop shacking up but I had to eat. Momma, that twin of yours be coming out all the time lol you can hide that side from others but I know she's there! I'm sure that is where I get my sarcastic side, and sassiness from.

Momma, you are my best blessing.

Mom, thank you for being steadfast and unmovable.

Sincerely, Edna (Your 3rd child)

Part Three

Overcoming for My Future

This time… I'm choosing me!

Listen to "I've Overcome" by Edna Sanders

Instructions:

Get your phone out, open your camera app, and point your camera toward my QR code below. Once the link comes up on your screen, just click it and go directly to the YouTube channel to hear this song. I want you to play this song while you read the section.

I'M AN OVERCOMER & IT'S MY TIME!
Author Edna Sanders

Journey of An Overcomer

Chapter Six
Changing My Mindset

As I write on this topic of changing my mindset, I am living through this, right this moment. I need these quotes and scriptures to get me out of this funky, mind place this morning. December 2022 was our first court date to hopefully finalize our divorce. Yeah, it didn't happen. I am acknowledging that: I am sad, hurt, and aggravated. Today is a hard day. I saw this quote, and I found myself.

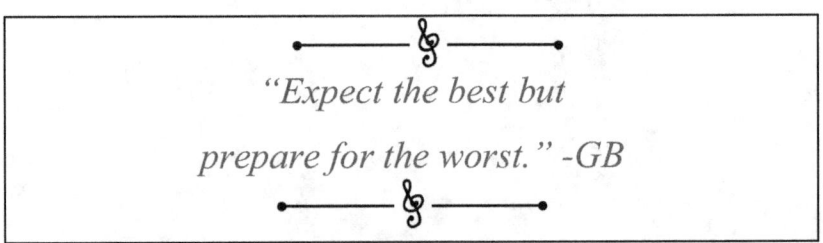

"Expect the best but prepare for the worst." -GB

Sad to say, but no, I didn't prepare for the worst... I went to court just hopeful that it would be over peacefully. I assumed maybe a hiccup

Journey of An Overcomer

here or there, but nothing that would break my soul, right? Look, my soul was broken!

Yeah, I let his words get to me…During court, it was said that I don't do anything alone for our children, and apparently, my children's dad and his support system do the majority of everything for our children. So yeah, I had a human experience, and the woman in me got emotional. Even though it was a lie, I let it get to me. It hurt me. Ya'll just those little words hurt me so badly. His words set me back mentally. Honestly, I had to snap out of it.

SUICIDAL THOUGHTS

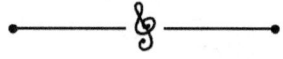

I have thought about death as a way-out numerous times, especially as a child when I encountered all of the abuse. I often thought that God made a mistake with me, and that he didn't need me in this family, but now, as a woman who is married with children, I face these same thoughts. I felt like DANG! Here I go again, messing up stuff. My children would be better off if I just let my husband, and his family raise our children. Yes, they may miss me for a year, but they don't need me. I'm just a place filler. My thoughts would ramble on, and I'd think things like they only need me when things are going bad, they are hurting, the house is dirty, or if bills need to be paid. I could not seem to satisfy my husband; I was always failing. I was like, really God! I try to be this and that for them, for my job, my family, and for friends, but I am only feeling used and broken. I am always failing them, somehow. Why am I here? I should just make life easier for them all and leave. I can say that my faith in God and my hope in Jesus during these times in my life are what helped me transform my thinking. The scripture Romans 12:2 says: "being transformed by the renewing of the mind." I know some people view this scripture in other ways. Yet for me this scripture just basically helped me change my thinking. When I changed my thinking, it helped me remember to laugh. I was retreating to my old, unhealthy, familiar routines. I began to:

- I let myself doubt myself again.
- I let myself second-guess my parenting. When I know that I am one Heck of a mom! When I know that I go above and beyond for all of my children, daily.
- I thought about giving him full custody and just disappearing.

Would anyone even notice that I am gone? Would anyone care?

- I thought, well, Dam, since what I do is not important around her, how about I swallow all these muscle relaxers and pain pills and go away forever.
- Thankfully, my cousin was nearby, and my "Super Pastor" called me right in time. I mean, it was like out of nowhere my phone rang, and it was Him. Hallelujah.

Joyce Meyer's Testimony has always touched me. She was raped and molested by her biological dad. If you haven't, you should go listen to her story. When I lived with my grandmother while going to college, I would listen to her often. I used to love reading back then. One day, my grandma got a gift from one of her children, and it included a book from Joyce Meyer.

The book I read was Battlefield of the Mind. I really enjoyed reading that book. During that season of my life, I was trying to grow stronger in my relationship with God. This book helped me see a woman who had gone through almost the exact same thing as I did, and I was in awe! I'm still amazed at how she managed to overcome abuse and divorce and still be as powerful as she is. So, yeah, I became a Joyce Meyer fan. But I am not writing about her just to admire her. There was one quote from her book that I focused on:

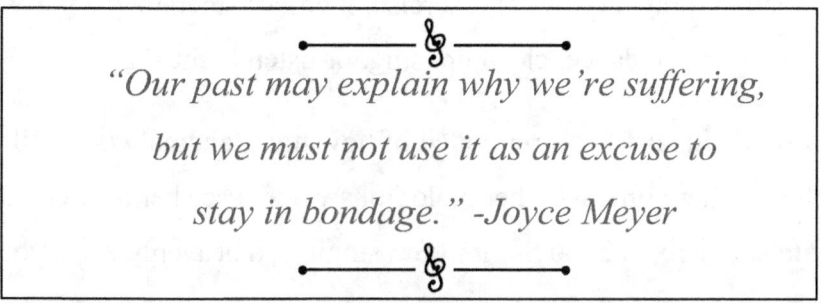

"Our past may explain why we're suffering, but we must not use it as an excuse to stay in bondage." -Joyce Meyer

As I am healing, I constantly have to speak to myself. I am reminded of how often many people would say a person is crazy for talking to themselves. Well, I disagree. Talking to myself has helped me change my mindset. As I read The Battlefield of the Mind and other scriptures and various quotes, I realize that I have to do what works for me. I am speaking over myself in this season. I am talking to myself and encouraging Edna. I speak various affirmations daily. I stop and correct myself when I think negatively about myself. See my past happened. Yet, I cannot let it hold me back anymore. I will face more obstacles and setbacks, but I cannot let those setbacks keep me stagnant. I must readjust. I must change my thinking instantly!

I am not sure how long you can dwell on a setback or a mistake, and I know the longer I sit and think negatively about a situation I retract and end up in a worse off situation. I have gotten sick and tired of being in that mindset. Therefore, I am doing something about it. My sisters and brothers do what you have to do to get out of that sunken place. I have made a list of some healthy options that you can use.

- Scream, pray, cry, write, exercise, meditate, therapist, counselor, call a friend, dance, clean up, sing, or listen to music, etc.

As I write this list, I am reminded of how my grandma would fill the atmosphere in her home with her melodious voice. I see her now cooking in the kitchen there on 2300 Summit St., singing so heavenly. As a young child, I would just listen and occasionally join in with her. As she is cooking or doing laundry and babysitting children, I am just relaxing and eating up her or grandpa's delicious food, messing up the house, I'm sure. I just didn't have a care or concern about anything. Just hearing her voice soothed me.

Yet as an adult with a house full of children, I find myself singing or humming around the house. I have noticed I do it to pour out my heart to

God about the unspoken request that I don't want to bother my children with. When I start, I am singing alone and possibly crying, then before I am finished my children have joined in with me and we may end up shouting and dancing around the house. Before I knew it, I was calm, and my focus and my mindset had changed instantly.

I can only imagine what concerns were on my grandma's heart. She sang just as boldly and just as anointed in the house full of us children as she would sing at a convention full of people. I am realizing that, yes, times have changed there are many ways people can get help for various mental and psychological issues or concerns. Please do what works for you. Listen, if you must go to the altar every time prayer is offered, do it! If you need a sabbatical and detach for a season, do it! If you must sit in your therapist's office every other day, child, do it! No matter what, if you must sing and cry or cry and sing, then do it! As we wake up and go to sleep every day and night, we all face our own mountains and hurdles. You, me, we, must ask ourselves Will this be my stopping point? Will I give up today? Yes, this situation broke my soul, but thank God I'm resilient! Thank God I've got some bounce back about me. I do believe that you have some bounce back inside of you, too.

Step back, breathe, change your thinking (you have a sound mind), do your strategy that works for you, trust God in you, and act out the plan.

Chapter Seven

Changing My Actions

Some of you may know that I have recently lost over one hundred pounds. The heaviest weight that I saw was 299 lbs. I am sure I was well over that before I went to the doctor because I had started walking a little bit, but I was way out of shape. I am short as it is, so I don't need any extra weight on this 5'0 frame. I am now down over 100lbs! I am not trying to lose weight now, I am trying to maintain and continue to eat healthier.

My goal is to transform how I cook for myself as well as how I cook for my children. It is easier said than done because the prices for healthy food for one person are outrageous, so just imagine what the prices for healthy food for a family of seven are! I had to make some changes in my lifestyle so I could be present for my children and especially myself. I did have a gastric bypass, which is how I lost most of my weight. Although before my surgery, I lost 30 lbs. on my own, walking and working out as often as I could. Y'all, I was/am proud of those 30 lbs. that I did on my own. I admit that my load in that season was strenuous, let me fill you in on a bit:

- a full 8hr workday,
- 6 children, (Cooking/cleaning)
- 4/6 children with disabilities,
- Adopting and bringing in 2 new children during COVID
- Getting my home ready for inspectors/and case workers
- Scheduling and taking children to never-ending Dr. Appt.'s
- Lupus flares
- Diabetes diagnoses
- High blood pressure
- Car getting repo'd
- Issues at work, with childcare, etc.
- Graduating with my associates degree, (Magna Cum Ladue)!!
- DHS investigations

Ya'll, the list goes on! I have/had a lot going on, that's not even half. I have decided to take control of my life and not let life take control of me. That's what was happening up above. As I write and read, I realize how chaotic it looks even as I write it. but living it was just as chaotic, and even worse. You are probably tripping on the fact that I said I am taking control of my life……funny. It's your choice to believe how you feel. I am doing what is best for me. I am doing what is best for my children and what is best for my future. I had to take action!

Taking action included...

- exercising daily, or at least 3-5 times a week/ walk/ yoga etc./ 30 min a day, something
- changing my eating (still working on it, but I'm doing it)
- stop doing things for others
- start doing things for myself
- being alone/separate from others your true people(tribe) will see about you
- Going to therapy/a mentor/close friend that will help you grow/pastor/etc.
- unlearning old habits/rituals
- learning myself
- Loving myself
- Focusing on the future/making a plan/acting on the plan
- Constantly thinking Godly/positive/ laughing, etc.
- Speak less, listen more
- Saying no, saying yes when needed/ learn to know the difference
- don't do things just because someone will be offended if I don't
- Love others from a distance
- Forgive others
- I had to forgive myself

I am sure many of you can and will find faults in my list of actions I took. I am still living, and I am sure I will either add or take away items as I feel necessary. I am trusting God to lead me on this journey. I have trusted others thus far, and my wayward thinking and I failed. I am trusting God to lead me on a clearer path that's less chaotic and stressful. I have faith that God is pleased because I am pleased with the steps I have been taking. I am God's daughter, and God is in me.

- Take action.
- Sit down somewhere quiet.
- Write out your day, month, etc.
- Ask yourself where can I make adjustments?
- Pray/Talk to yourself/God (whatever you do)

Do it., Live it (your life), and enjoy it.

My Letter to Myself

Dear Edna,

The Broken Carefree Teenager

Hey, lil' carefree, sweet, and broken Edna Sanders. You did not know how life was going to turn you for a loop. All you wanted to do was laugh and play. Yeah, Lil Edna, you made a few mistakes here and there, but it's nothing to keep your head down about.

See, my dear Edna, you did tell that one teacher shut up in pre-school, and you may have signed one D-Hall slip too many. You may even run your mouth at times, whereas you should have been quiet. Yeah, baby, it's a part of life, and more mistakes are ahead. Listen, sometimes what you think is your weakness is your strength....... just a lil' nugget as you grow. Oh, yea, even when that old man rubbed up your leg on the church van when you were too young to even know what was going on.... yeah, it's sad, you want to tell someone, but who can you trust? Will they hurt you too, now that your daddy did it, you can't trust anyone.... but don't let it break you. You have a purpose.

You have overcome this, and get ready, baby, you're about to overcome even more.

Mrs Edna Reid,

Newly Married Mother Broken and Damaged

So, you see what I said about there's more to come... I wish I could have warned you. I wish I could have given you a heads up. I wish I could have run into the future to hold you. This is a tough season for you. You are recently married, and you just informed your family of all the painful things that your dad did to you. I know so many didn't believe you. So many said you deserved it, so many said that you should never have spoken about it. But they must have forgotten about the Lil' Edna, I remember as a little girl who said too much. Don't cry too much about your dad not walking you down the aisle for your wedding, you love hard, but soon enough, you will only want in your life those who want you... This season is not the end.... Oh me, oh my! If I can tell you one thing about the future, that voice is only going to get more powerful the more you grow. That's all I can tell you about what is to come. Girl, you are strong!

It was not your fault! You are responsible for your actions, as He and anyone else are responsible for their own actions. As you are for your decisions thus far……. Yes, you're thinking now as you're pregnant with your 2nd child and your husband calls you to tell you that "I let a woman in the house, and she sat on his lap, but nothing happened" (I made my bed I have to lay in it) No you don't!! Hell pulls the sheets off that bed and makes it another way, while you're at it get a whole new bed and through that one out!! Oh, but you are still loving, giving, and there for everyone!!! Do you realize that you have gained so much weight? No,

Edna, not the physical weight………... that mental weight, baby. Keep living it out, because your Exodus is coming…

Ms. Sanders,

Divorced and Healed

SOOO, look what you made it through. It has not been easy, but this has been a journey; 37 years and counting. I have a question for you, Ms. Sanders. You have forgiven everyone associated with your pain. You have forgiven your dad; you have forgiven your Ex-husband. I get it….

I forgive you for not believing in you. I forgive you for loving others, but not yourself. but could you really give them an authentic love when you really didn't know what love was? Give yourself grace, I did my best at that time. I loved from what I knew love to be. I know better now. I am going to do better. I forgive myself from negative thinking and speaking negatively about myself. When negative thoughts come, I will quickly replace them with positive thoughts. I forgive myself for wallowing in my weaknesses. I am strong now, and I have always been. I will continue to be strong as I am a model for my children. They have a strong black mother who has endured many obstacles: mental, physical, and spiritual. This is not the end. I will have new obstacles and various mountains to climb. But I know I won't hinder myself.

Phil. 4:13 "I can do all things through Christ, which strengthens me." I got this.

I forgive myself for not caring for my temple as I should have. I make a vow to cherish and love this vessel that God has blessed me with. I am excited to walk in this new, forgiven and healed version of Edna!

Tributes

I want to acknowledge God, my creator. I am this strong person because of how God made me. I am thankful for ME…. I went through this, and I will be better for myself and all of my loved ones.

First, My Children:

Braisly, you are so strong; I admire the confidence in you. You have so much ambition, and I hope that I can help you blossom into who you and God want you to be. Continue to love yourself. Yes, Queen Braisly... you are truly majestic. No, you weren't breathing initially at birth, but honey! We can't tell, (lol) You beat us talking!! Lol, you're definitely a social butterfly. Hopefully, you meet your goal of public speaking to some degree.

Kinslee, my sweet, powerful girl. You are helping me to enhance my parenting style. You are thoughtful, and you think of everyone. You help me remember to care about the things I might not consider a priority, such as animals, nature, art, etc. You are a protector, you remind me of me when I was younger. You are such a protector of your siblings.

Charity Girl, you Rock! You are one brilliant and beautiful little lady. Yes, you keep me on my toes. You might be the family clown because you always keep me fussing or laughing. Thank you for being super independent and wanting to do everything yourself. But child, let me help you (sometimes). But never stop being strong, funny, and brilliant.

Trinity, my mighty mix of a soldier-sheep, was my perfect gift at such a chaotic time in my life. You are a rea of sunshine. I smile at how anxious you are to assist and add your input on everything. You love to stand up for others and I love that about you. You are a sweetheart and a firecracker all in one.

To Daniel Reid III. My son-shine! Thank you so much for being a sweet peace in the house full of craziness. You are so smart. You learn so fast. You are also an encourager. Often, you will say "I love you, mommy!" and you'll run up and kiss me on my cheek. You give me numerous reasons to smile. I love how helpful and positive you are. I learn from your calmness.

Then my Patrick (Pat-Pat), the boss man, you remind me why I have to keep working, lol because you can put away some food. But seriously, Pat you are my reminder that boys need just as much TLC as any girl. You are also a quiet storm, lol. My soft-spoken guy will fight in heartbeat, pray saints! Although I do know anytime that the weather looks scary and the thunder roars, Patrick is on his way to snuggle with his mommy.

To My Family:

My Grandmom (Ercille Devine), My parents, My (Super) Pastor Bishop Withers, My siblings: Darrell Jr (Tamika), Kimberly Bankston (Antwan), Samuel Sanders (Lannayah), Mary Sanders, and Jairus Sanders (Ashley), my nephews, nieces, aunts, uncles, and cousins. Thank you for your patience with my transformation and the seeds you have sown in my life.

Friends:

A word I use scarcely, but these three are close to being my representation of The Holy Trinity in the flesh, lol, (don't crucify me): Geoffrey Biggs, Angelia McGhee, and Klassic Harper; Thank you all so much. I don't have the proper words to express how grateful I am to have you three in my life. You have all been real deal-Holyfield, absolutely the best people ever!

THE JOURNEY OF AN OVERCOMER

BONUS CONTENT

Here's a list of things I've had to heal from and I'm healing through. Join me on this healing journey!

GOD IS WITH YOU

THE JOURNEY OF AN OVERCOMER
BORN TO OVERCOME

PEOPLE PLEASING
I excessively focused on making others happy at the expense of my wants and needs.

WALKING IN OFFENSE
I was easily offended by others and situations that occurred.

OVER EATING
Overeating is eating past the point of fullness. When we overeat, we eat even though we aren't hungry. If it becomes a habit, overeating can lead to weight gain. I did this often!

LOW SELF-ESTEEM
I was extremely critical of myself, ignoring positive qualities.

LONELINESS
I had a fear of being alone, dying alone and being unloved. Well now I enjoy my alone time! Actually the more time I spend alone the closer I get to God. Being a single mother of six rambunctious children removed all of my loneliness fears. I crave my moments of solitude. Yeah even without a husband. I am happy, fulfilled and content in this season. Loneliness will not force me into a relationship ever.

STAGNANCY
A state of inactivity, lack of progress or movement, and lack of change or development. It often implies a period of no growth or improvement,

PHYSICALLY
My heaviest weight was 300 with a 5'1 frame. I move now! I love to move, now at 196 lbs.

CREATIVELY
I would sit down on my own creativity and boost everyone.

PHYSICAL SEXUAL ABUSE
There was so much that this trauma caused and contributed to. It was the root of everything else I needed to heal from!

EMOTIONAL SEXUAL ABUSE
I was a child whose emotions were stifled and buried alive. Losing my virginity the way I did still eats at me

LACK OF ACCOUNTABILITY
I was guilty of blaming others for mistakes, not following through on commitments, and avoiding responsibility.

SELF RIGHTEOUS

Life humbled me and I sat down somewhere. I listened to God, while observing my life and then made changes (mentally/spiritually). I began helping others from a pure, non-judgmental heart. (I also found scriptures and life quotes on these topics and applied them to my life.)

FEAR OF FAILURE

Someone once said… "If at first you don't succeed, try, try again" (I also found scriptures and life quotes on these topics and applied them to my life.)

FEAR OF SUCCESS

I didn't even realize this was a thing until one of my aunties on my mom's side brought this to my attention years ago (Aunt Rocky!) Who would be fearful of actually succeeding in life? Me! My God, I'm currently slowly overcoming this even now! I'm so comfortable in the background, and/or behind the scenes. (I also found scriptures and life quotes on these topics and applied them to my life.)

FEAR OF RELATIATION

I was fearful of the repercussions of speaking up for people and standing up against people/companies who had more power (ex. employers, teachers, family elders, and church leaders etc.) What is your why? What are you adamite about? My best friend (GB!) tells me all the time "Stand on it!" To overcome this fear… if you are advocating for your or others' rights and/or beliefs you may need to find your "I don't care" bone somewhere; and "stand on it!!" (Find your method and do it).

MURDEROUS THOUGHTS / ANGER

(I found scriptures and life quotes on these topics and applied them to my life.) Changing my mindset and laughing help with this.

MISUSE OF PRESCRIPTION

In Jr high, I used my inhaler and liked the silly feeling it gave me. I eventually got diagnosed with dangerously strong pain meds for lupus and I had to listen to God regarding taking my meds. I refused to take my meds to avoid getting addicted and now I don't even need them for lupus. I knew I didn't want anything controlling me. I have a natural/spiritual high!

NEGATIVE THINKING

I am still quoting various affirmations and scripture to help me with this on a daily basis.

DEPRESSION

I took control of my life and the situations... I have taken on the saying wholeheartedly. "My peace is more important"... More than any job or relationship. I get sad, sure I do but it's only for a season. Ecclesiastes talks about seasons and times... I definitely prefer praising and singing over sadness...I sing/dance/ walk/ pray etc. through it all.

PTSD

Many things have aided in this diagnosis of PTSD, but I am overcoming as I write to you... and help you. In children's therapy, please go, also learn to find reasons to have good laughing and crying sessions.... Find me, I'll laugh and cry with you (depending on the day) (lol)

HIGH BLOOD PRESSURE

Getting divorced helped my number come down, but also working in a stressful environment during it aided in my levels rising again and causing me to have a very scary emergency hospital visit. I am overcoming this by maintaining my stress levels, walking, exercising, mountain climbing etc.

DIABETES

I was diagnosed with it back in Spring of 2021. I didn't need meds, just monitored through proper eating and working out. Although now its not ever registering!! Hallelujah!

LUPUS

Since 2007 I was diagnosed with lupus and I was put on a daily high dose of steroids and various other meds!!! Thankfully since 2022 it's been in remission and not registering whenever they draw blood. My Dr. has me off all lupus meds and I love it. To God be the Glory! (I'm so excited!)

GENERATIONAL CURSES

Debt, secrets, mentalities, fears, any/all that apply. I'm focused on destroying it!

SELF HATE

I had an intense pervasive feeling of disgust and hatred for myself. I also faced extreme body image issues due to drastic body changes, along with my bypass surgery in March of 2022) I didn't even like to look in the mirror due to the fact I felt like I look too much like my dad.

NOTES: What are you healing from?

AUTHOR EDNA SANDERS

POISONOUS LOVE

This guy that I know is one of a kind. Since I was so young, his words engulfed my mind. Yeah, I was too young to know what love was or what it meant, but it was something there, a peace, a calmness, but I'm not exactly sure. I was too busy, too wild, too free; whatever that love thing was, it could stay far away from me. The more we grew, the more I knew it was something to this guy I knew. He's different, unique, a little aggravating, but dang-it! I like the way he thinks! I can't call it love.. no, not yet, I'm way too young to feel like that. Although the more we talk, the more we laugh, the more we'd joke and smile, Idk... I'm thinking it just might be worth my while!

Oh, no, not this little girl, "child, you need to wait a while."

Before I knew it, I was like a teen, and those feelings for him never ended. Although no one knew the pain I'd endure, so much hurt, so much sadness, so much shame was my name.... Being raped by a preacher, my dad! Words he'd say are "You've got to learn how to submit!" It had become so routine; I would eat away my pain, promising myself that I'd never submit to a man... My only escape was my friend, the guy I knew.... No, he didn't know what I went through. If you recall, I had to make everyone believe I was so wild and free! Oh, no; he couldn't love me. Then, just like that, my thoughts became my words, and my words became life. Now look, hey, congrats on your girl, she looks nice.

 Staying in my lane is a skill I acquired to protect myself from this love I desired. I had to treat him like a shrimp. Yeah, so sad, I know; but well, shrimp if consumed or too close to my skin will hurt me; That's what I felt every time we'd connect, but another girl had his hand and heart. It felt so toxic to want him. It hurt so bad to love him, to see someone else be with him. Yet we connected even more, without a kiss, barely a hug, or a held hand. I had to avoid this poisonous love.

AUTHOR EDNA SANDERS

CONTINUATION

Well, this guy that I knew grew finer and wiser. He'd grown to be so prudent and still extremely calming. Anytime I was near him, there was a peace they say you only find in Jesus……If that's the truth, why do I find it with you? I almost relaxed my charade the day you took my breath away with a deep gaze in your eyes. I swear I could have submitted to him! Yet, the fear of the pain of not being thin enough, cute enough, or smart enough, I maintained my charade, I stayed in my lane, and well ... Thanks for coming to my wedding, I guess..

 After fifteen years of being engulfed with my life and pretending to be a happy wife, one would assume that my heart had changed... that's where it becomes painful! The pain of having loved and still loving, the pain of my choices, the pain of not loving myself enough to heal before I changed my last name, and the pain of not listening to that prudent man. And then I reappear, and you help me heal. My God, man! Who are you? Giving me scriptures and quotes, helping me unlearn and relearn, walking me through healing exercises, patiently listening to me hour after hour, helping me notice the Goddess within, as you continue to ignore my shameful advances towards you. Yeah, even now, I may say I'm reliving the pain of not being chosen, again, and again, and it started to hurt. But this time around, I've changed my perspective….Yes, the desire to submit to that prudent man (the guy I knew) has multiplied tremendously.

Although now I desire more to get reacclimated with that little girl who was so wild and so free….and never to lose her again... all I see is healing now, and that poisonous love has faded away.

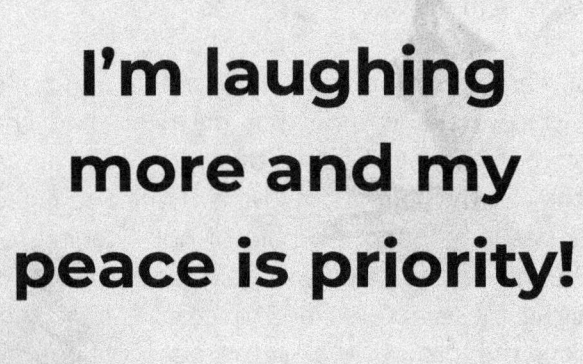

Professional Acknowledgements

Book Publisher/Editor:
Living Waters Book Publishing Co.

Cover photo credit photographer:
Ashley Sanders

Makeup Artist:
Casey Simmons

Music Producer:
Marquis "Boo" Blake

Background Vocalist:
Bethany Devine, Mary Sanders, Jairus Sanders

Music Graphics: Klassic Harper

JOURNEY OF AN OVERCOMER

AUTHOR BIOGRAPHY

I am the mother of six wonderful children. They are my motivation, and they also keep me on my toes—trust me, there's never a dull moment when you have six children around. I work a full-time job, and I consistently have the mindset that I am going to put my children in a better position in life.

I once heard, "You know you have found your calling or purpose in life when you find a career that you could/would do for free." This is how I feel about my career as one of the victim advocates at Percy and Donna Malone Child Safety Center. Every day, I find myself helping families near and far, and of course, it's a plus that I get paid to do what I love to do. I have also worked for over 20+ years as an Early Childhood Development Professional. For the past eleven years, I worked as one of the Lead Education Technicians for the Department of Defense on the Little Rock Air Force Base.

Working with children and families of many different ages and abilities, from all over the world, has taught this little country girl from Malvern, Arkansas, many wonderful things. I've learned to be a mother by observing so many of the mothers I've worked with. I have learned that each child has a unique way of learning. I learned from each child, and working with them consistently teaches me how to be a better nurturer to my children.

After being a survivor of poly-victimization, my desire to advocate for victims and families of abuse has grown tremendously. I am a voice for the voiceless and a guiding light in a dark place. I am the "helps" that was mentioned in the Bible...(1 Corinthians 12:28) No, I don't have to have a big title before or after my name... "a helper" is fine with me.

JOURNEY OF AN OVERCOMER

★★★★★

"YOU HAVE SUCH A POWERFUL STORY WITHIN YOU FROM GOD"

LIVING WATER BOOKS

OFFICE NUMBER
501-488-0031
Livingwaterbooks.org
Livingwaters@livingwaterbooks.org

LIVING WATER BOOKS PUBLISHING

PUBLISHING CO

www.ingramcontent.com/pod-product-compliance
Lightning Source LLC
Chambersburg PA
CBHW061419300426
44114CB00015B/1990